IBS International Summer

Wolfram Hardt
Uranchimeg Tudevdagva
(Hrsg.)

I0019070

TUD*press*

IBS Scientific Workshop Proceedings

Herausgegeben von Stiftung IBS, Wolfram Hardt

Band 2

IBS International Summer School

Wolfram Hardt
Uranchimeg Tudevdagva
(Hrsg.)

TUDpress

2015

Bibliografische Information der Deutschen Nationalbibliothek
Die Deutsche Nationalbibliothek verzeichnet diese Publikation in der
Deutschen Nationalbibliografie; detaillierte bibliografische Daten sind im
Internet über http://dnb.d-nb.de abrufbar.

Bibliographic information published by the Deutsche Nationalbibliothek
The Deutsche Nationalbibliothek lists this publication in the Deutsche Nationalbibliografie; detailed bibliographic data are available in the Internet
at http://dnb.d-nb.de.

ISBN 978-3-95908-023-1

© 2015 TUDpress
Verlag der Wissenschaften GmbH
Bergstr. 70 | D-01069 Dresden
Tel.: 0351/47 96 97 20 | Fax: 0351/47 96 08 19
http://www.tudpress.de

IBS Annual Summer School

Foundation IBS supports the establishment, growth and preservation of scientific oriented interdisciplinary networks. National and international scientists and experts are brought together for research and technology transfer, where the foundation IBS provides the suitable environment for conferences, workshops and seminars. Especially young researchers are encouraged to join all IBS events.

The series *IBS Scientific Workshop Proceedings (IBS-SWP)* publishes peer reviewed papers contributed to IBS - Workshops. IBS-SWP are open access publications, i.e. all volumes are online available at IBS website www.ibs-laubuch.de/ibs-swp and free of charge.

IBS Scientific Workshop Proceedings aim at the ensuring of permanent visibility and access to the research results presented during the events staged by Foundation IBS.

Preface

Annual summer school was organized successful in this year from 29th June to 1th July in Laubusch, Germany. In this summer school attended bachelor, master and doctors students, researchers from Mongolia, Germany, Russia, India and Turkey. Topics of SS2015 were: e-learning, embedded systems and international cooperation between universities of partner countries.

One of the highlighted points of this year was attendance of bachelor students from Mongolia and video session with Russian delegation. Master students from India and Turkey presented own ongoing research and got live feedback from researchers and professors.

Next highlight of summer school was formal agreement with extension of Summer School in next year by Harbin Technical University, China. By idea of Russian university summer school will be change places from year to year by partner university countries.

One of the main goals of this international event is to give opportunity to students and researchers of partner universities to work together during school time actively and freely in frame if science and international cooperation. By feedback of participants this goal are reaching well and we are glad that this idea extending from year to year by different countries.

Editorial Board

Prof. Uranchimeg Tudevdagva
Mongolian University of Science and Technology Ulaanbaatar

Kati Pügner, M.A.
Technische Universität Chemnitz

Prof. Dr. Wolfram Hardt, Editor-in-Chief
Technische Universität Chemnitz, Stiftung IBS

www.ibs-laubusch.de/ibs-swp

IBS Scientific Workshop Proceedings

IBS Summerschool June 29th to July 1st 2015

Table of contents

H.264 Video Streaming on Embedded Platform Using Wireless Network 3
Sodkhuu Dalaikhuu, Uyangaa Khuchit, Khurelbaatar Tseveenjav,
Damdinsuren Bayanduuren

Design and Implementation of Medical Android Tablet featuring Zigbee 6
B. Enkhbat, D. Otgonbat, D. Enkhzul, T. Amartuvshin, Ts. Khurelbaatar,
B. Luubaatar, T. Enhkbaatar

Observer Regulation for Energy-Efficient Group-Value Applications 10
Daniel Reißner, Wolfram Hardt

Future Development of Mobile 5G Technology in Mongolia, Its Network Planning 13
Yura Otgonbaatar, Uranchimeg Tudevdagva

The Automatic Diagnostic by Pulse Based on the Expert System 19
Yumchmaa Ayush, Grif M. G., Uranchimeg Tudevdagva

Aspects of Computer Sign Language Interpretation System Development 23
Yuliya S. Manueva

Sensor Integration in Multi-Channel Measurement System Based on 26
The Inverse or The Wiener Filter
Julia S. Petrova, Alexander A. Spector

Hardware Accelerated Sensing for Fault Detection and Safety Assessment 29
of Turbo Generators
Yanjin Altankhuyag

Development of Wireless PGN Analyzer for ISOBUS Network 33
Enkhbaatar Tumenjargal, Luubaatar Badarch, Woonchul Ham, Enkhzul Doopalam,
Amartuvshin Togooch

International Accreditation on Bachelor's and Master's Degree programmes 39
Sergelen Byambaa, Batchimeg Tserenchoijil, Angar Sharkhuu

The E-Learning and Virtual Laboratory in Engineering Education on 43
The Example of MUST
Uranchimeg Tudevdagva

MOOC from The View of Students 46
Oyudari Lkha-Ochir, Nomindari Lkha-Ochir

H.264 Video Streaming on Embedded Platform Using Wireless Network

Sodkhuu Dalaikhuu, Uyangaa Khuchit, Khurelbaatar Tseveenjav, Damdinsuren Bayanduuren
Department of Electronics, School of Information and Communication Technology
Mongolian University of Science and Technology
Ulaanbaatar, Mongolia
sodkhuu@ametrossolutions.com, khurelbaatar@sict.edu.mn, damdinsurenb@must.edu.mn

Abstract—We present the design and implementation of computer vision-based person following mobile robot using wireless network and embedded platform. The Binocular Sparse Feature Segmentation (BSFS) algorithm is implemented in order to determine the location of the person in the image and thereby control the robot. Unlike other computer vision-based approaches, the mobile robot is not required to load high performance computers on itself while embedded platform is implemented for streaming the video sequences via wireless network to the fixed-site computer. The computer executes BSFS algorithm on the received video sequences and responds control commands to the mobile robot. The Exynos4412 based embedded platform is used as the mobile robot controlling board.

Keywords—embedded platform; wireless networks; computer vision; image processing;

I. INTRODUCTION

In recent years, various kinds of applications has achieved great development with the rapid convergence of embedded platforms, wireless communication technologies and image processing technologies. Computer vision based mobile robot is one of such implementations. Various applications would benefit from such a capability, including security robots that detect and follow intruders, interactive robots, and service robots that must follow a person to provide continual assistance. Thus, we are interested in developing security robots for detecting and following intruders with this work.

In [1], person following with a mobile robot using binocular feature-based tracking algorithm has been introduced. The Binocular Sparse Feature Segmentation (BSFS) is based upon matching sparse Lucas-Kanade features, in a binocular stereo system. It detects and matches feature points between a stereo pair of images and between successive images in the sequence in order to track 3D points in time. Comparing to the color-based approaches, this method does not require the person to wear clothing with different color from the background environment. In our system, we used this algorithm for person detecting and tracking.

Comparison of several well known optical flow estimation results has been introduced in [2]. Results are presented for many of the well known optical flow estimation methods, including those from Horn and Schunck, Anandan, Lucas and Kanade, and Singh, Fleet and Jepson, Obobez and Bouthemy,

Uras et al., and Nagel. The experiments has been done in several kinds of motion pictures such as tree, yosemite, taxi, and flower garden etc. The program execution time of Lucas and Kanade method was the least, only 9 seconds, which is suitable for our real-time wireless communicating system. The comparison of the program execution time for each of the presented methods is shown in TABLE I. Also, others results for all sequences has been decent. For example, the comparative results for the Taxi sequence is shown in TABLE II.

TABLE I. PROGRAM EXECUTION TIME FOR EACH OF THE PRESENTED METHODS

Method	Execution Time/minutes:seconds
Anandan	3:26
Fleet and Jepson	45:15
Horn and Schunck	0:54
Lucas and Kanade	0:09
Motion Trajectory Based	35:12
Nagel	1:54
Odobez and Bouthemy	0:39
Singh (Step 1, n=2, w=3)	4:37
Singh (Step 2, n=2, w=2)	7:08
Uras et, Al.	0:12

TABLE II. COMPARATIVE RESULTS FOR THE TAXI SEQUENCE

Algorithm	Mean error	Standard Deviation	Density (%)
Motion Trajectory Based	3.67	2.92	100
Odobez and Bouthemy	3.93	3.17	98.87
Lucas and Kanade	3.99	3.23	100
Horn and Schunck (modified)	4.01	3.25	100
Nagel	4.21	3.48	100

1

Algorithm	Mean error	Standard Deviation	Density (%)
Motion Trajectory Based	3.67	2.92	100
Anandan	4.35	3.60	100

In this paper we present the design and implementation of computer vision-based person following robot using wireless network and embedded platform. The system utilizes a) ARM Cortex 9 based board with embedded linux operating system for mobile robot control; b) Lucas-Kanade feature detection based Binocular Sparse Feature Segmentation algorithm for automatic person detection and tracking; c) wireless video streaming technology using H.264 codec for remote controlling and monitoring;

II. SYSTEM OVERVIEW

The system architecture is shown in Fig. 1. When robot detects motion by it's camera, it starts streaming H.264 coded video to the fixed-site computer. The computer executes BSFS image processing algorithm on the received video sequences and responds control commands to the robot.

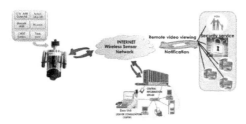

Fig. 1. System architecture

Fig. 2. Mobile robot control system architecture

The robot control system is designed with a modular hardware structure completely. The main control board of the robot is based on exynos4412 CPU module with ARM Cortex A9 processor. The peripheral circuit includes 2GB DDR3 RAM, EMMC 16GB flash memory, Ethernet interface circuit, RS-232 interface control circuit, I2C serial interface circuit, clock circuit, reset circuit, power module, external circuit and so on. Realtek RTL188EUS is used as wireless communication module. Two OV5640 rear 5 mega pixel omnivision cameras are used for image capturing. Atmega128 microcontroller based Arduino development board is used for controlling robot motor driving circuit. The robot control system architecture is shown in Fig. 2. Implementation

III. SYSTEM IMPLEMENTATION AND EXPERIMENTS

In order to test the proposed system, we have implement OpenCV based software on embedded linux platform whi streams two camera video to the fixed-site computer. T BSFS algorithm was implemented in Visual C++ on a So VAIO E17 laptop (2.20 GHz). Intel's OpenCV library was us for the feature detection, feature tracking, and face detectic The maximum driving speed of the robot was 0.5 meters p second, while the maximum turning speed was 30 degrees p second.

The system has been tested in indoor environment with types of size and quality between 100%, 70%, 50%, 20% a 5%. Fig. 3 and 4 shows the Lucas-Kanade based featu detection results on two different quality. In Fig. 3, the result streaming with 100% quality is shown. As it shows, 85 featu points are detected, mainly on the person. It is fair f successfully following the person. In Fig. 4, the result streaming 20% quality is shown. When quality is reduced, becomes noisy with over 100 false feature points.

Fig. 3. Feature detection from streaming video with 100% quality

Fig. 4. Feature detection from streaming video with 20% quality

The video streaming wireless network speed is measur by Color Bandwidth Meter, Linux command line tool. / shown in Fig. 5 and Fig. 6, 10% quality video streamii transmit network bandwidth was approximately 107.10 kB and 100% quality video streaming bandwidth w approximately 202.04 kB/s. The relation between the netwo bandwidth and the streaming video quality is shown in the Fi 7.

Fig. 5. 10% quality video streaming network bandwidth

Fig. 6. 100% quality video streaming network bandwidth

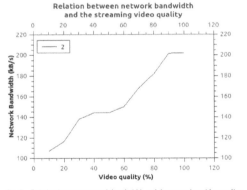

Fig. 7. Relation between network bandwidth and the streaming video quality

IV. CONCLUSION AND FUTURE WORK

We introduced an implementation of wireless video streaming on embedded platform. The proposed system works in indoor environment. The BSFS algorithm is implemented for person following purpose. This method is based upon matching sparse Lucas-Kanade features, in binocular stereo system. Unlike the color-based approaches, this method does not require the person to wear clothing with different color from the background. The wireless video streaming is implemented by H.264 coded video. Uncompressed video takes so much storage space and transmission bandwidth that video compression provides an effective approach to save the space and bandwidth. Also, we have tested reducing the size and quality of the video to determine the minimum video streaming data for the proposed system. In result, the minimum video streaming quality for our system is 30% quality video. The further reduction makes too much noisy background with makes person detection unstable even though network bandwidth becomes very low. We are planning to implement variable-bit rate algorithm for the future development. Adaptivity is one of the most important features for applications in wireless systems to react to the dynamics due to statistical traffic, variable receiving conditions, as well as handovers and random user activity. Also, the purposed wireless video streaming and image processing system environment is suitable for various application development such as for the traffic surveillance system which detects and counts vehicles and trajectory tracking for one selected vehicle. The embedded platform and wireless technology enables integrating multiple cameras to the system with low cost and easy installing process.

REFERENCES

[1] Zhichao Chen and Stanley T. Birchfield, "Person Following with a Mobile Robot Using Binocular Feature-Based Tracking," IEEE/RSJ International Conference on Intelligent Robots and Systems (IROS), San Diego, California, October 2007

[2] David Gibson and Micheal Spann, "Robust Optical Flow Estimation Based on a Sparse Motion Trajectory Set," IEEE transactions on image processing, vol. 12, no. 4, April 2003

[3] www.opencv.org

[4] Fan Yunsheng, Guo Chen, Zhang Chuang, "The Research of Embedded Ships Video Wireless Transmission Control System," Proceedings of 2009 Conference on Communication Faculty

[5] R.Susanto, D.Wu, X.Lin, K.P.Lim, R.Yu, F.Pan, Z.Li, S.Yao, G.Feng, S.Wu, "Live Video Streaming on Embedded Devices through Wireless Channel," Signal Processing Program, Laboratories for Information Technology

[6] Dolley Shukla, Ekta Patel, "Speed Determination of Moving Vehicles using Lucas-Kanade Algorithm," International Journal of Computer Applications Technology and Research, vol 2, issue 1, 32-36, 2003, ISSN:2319-8656

[7] M Naga Raju, Prof. Bharadwaj Amrutur, "Battery Operated Wireless Video Surveillance System," a project report submitted in partial fulfilment of the requirements for the Degree of Master of Engineering in Faculty of Engineering, Department of Electrical Communication Engineering, Indian Institute of Science, Bangalore, June 2013

[8] Xiaoqing Zhu, Bernd Girod, "Video Streaming over Wireless Networks," Information Systems Laboratory, Stanford University.

Design and Implementation of Medical Android Tablet featuring Zigbee

Sodkhuu D., Bayar Ts., Tserendavaa O., Batkholboo N., Ganzorig N., Tulgabaatar D.,
Research and Development Center
Ametros Solutions LLC
Philadelphia PA, USA
{sodkhuu,bayar,batkholboo}@ametrossolutions.com

Enkhbat B., Otgonbat D., Enkhzul D., Amartuvshin T., Khurelbaatar Ts., Luubaatar B., Enhkbaatar T.,
Department of Electronic Engineering, SICT,
Mongolian University of Science and Technology
Ulaanbaatar, Mongolia
{enkhzul,amartuvshin,khurelbaatar,enkhbaatar}@must.edu.
mn

Abstract—This paper serves as an introduction to design and development of medical android tablet implementing Zigbee technology. Nowadays, there are wide spread use of information technology products, including PCs, notebooks and tablet PCs, in clinical environment. However, they have severe limitations in mobility, cost and custom development possibilities. This device offers the advantages of existing technology while simultaneously eradicating the aforementioned limitations. Texas Instrument's CC2530 based Zigbee module, the Samsung Exynos4412 ARM Cortex-A9 quad cores embedded processor and Android 4.4 KitKat operating system are utilized in the device. Furthermore, it has an integrated patient registration, monitoring and management system.

Keywords—Embedded Android; medical tablet; embedded processor; Zigbee;

I. INTRODUCTION

The rapid development of information technology and competition within the medical industry has brought us to the development of mobile medical devices. The 'hospitalized-placed' nurse has more demand than other medical workers [1]. Nowadays, a trend in medical digital convergence is to develop embedded systems integrated with application programs and web server based systems such as Desktop PCs, Tablet PCs and so on. In recent years, 'Hospitalized-placed' nurses use Windows platform based Desktop PCs and Tablet PCs the most. Their main functions are to search, check data, record medical care action and so on. The characteristics of Tablet PCs, Notebooks, PDAs and PC are shown in Table 1 [1]. It shows that Tablet PCs have better functions in terms of mobility, carry-on and touch panel than Desktop PCs, and are higher on functions such as peripheral integration, writing recognition and battery capacity than PDAs. Moreover, they place emphasis on file security and user-friendly interfaces, which means the Tablet PC has marketability with regards to medical applications. However, most medical Tablet PCs are expensive and based on Windows platform, which makes it harder for further development.

On the other hand, nurses and physicians are unable to frequently enter medical information into Desktop PCs or research patients' information and record immediately whilst taking care of patients. This condition not only causes inconvenience for nurses and physicians but also influences the accuracy of anamnesis, and subsequently decreases the quality of the treatment.

TABLE I.   COMPARISON OF TABLET PC, NOTEBOOK, PDA AND PC

Characteristics	Tablet PC	Notebook	PDA	PC
Operating System	Same as PC	Same as PC	Different with PC	x
Wireless	Very good	Very good	Hard	Very good
Mobile	Very good	Common	Good	Hard
Carry-On	Very good	Good	Very good	Hard
Touch panel	Very good	Good	Very good	No
Peripheral Integration	Very good	Very good	Hard	Very good
Writing recognition	Very good	No	Common	No
Battery capacity	Common	Common	Good	Very good
File security	Very good	Very good	Common	Common
Interfaces	Very good	Common	Hard	Common

Herein, we present a tablet that combines resolves these issues. The tablet offers a possibility to improve treatment quality through a quick information access for nurses and physicians.

II. SYSTEM DESIGN

The proposed tablet features a system that integrates direct clinical processes, such as patient registration and monitoring, with management processes. Figure 1 shows the structure of the hardware architecture of mobile clinical android tablet.

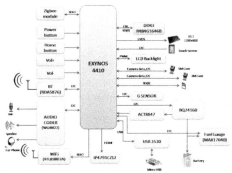

Fig. 1. Structure of the hardware architecture of mobile clinical android tablet.

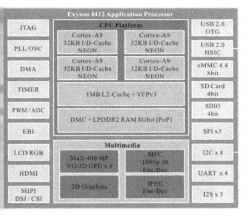

Exynos 4412 Application Processor			
JTAG	CPU Platform		USB 2.0 OTG
PLL/OSC	Cortex-A9 32KB I/D-Cache NEON	Cortex-A9 32KB I/D-Cache NEON	USB 2.0 HSIC
DMA	Cortex-A9 32KB I/D-Cache NEON	Cortex-A9 32KB I/D-Cache NEON	eMMC 4.4 8bit
TIMER	1MB L2-Cache + VFPv3		SD Card 4bit
PWM/ADC	DMC + LPDDR2 RAM 8Gbit (PoP)		SDIO 4bit
EBI			SPI x3
	Multimedia		
LCD RGB	Mali-400 MP VG/3D GPU x 4	MFC 1080p 30 Enc/Dec	I2C x 8
HDMI	2D Graphics	JPEG Enc/Dec	UART x 4
MIPI DSI / CSI			I2S x 3

Fig. 2. Exynos 4412 application processor architecture.

A. Embedded Processor

In order to port Android platform, Samsung Exynos 4 Quad core (4412) which is an ARM Cortex-A9 based application processor has been used. Exynos is a series of ARM-based System-on-Chips (SoCs) by Samsung Electronics, and is a continuation of Samsung's earlier S3C, S5L and S5P line of SoCs [2].

This branch CPU has been used widely in electronics products, such as Samsung Galaxy S II, Samsung Galaxy Tab 7.0 Plus, Samsung Galaxy Note, Samsung Galaxy Tab 7.0 and many more. Figure 1 shows the architecture of Exynos 4412 application processor.

Since Exynos 4412 chip includes interfaces for camera, audio codec, LAN, HDMI, and micro SD-card, it is easy to equip a module with various devices.

B. Android Open Source Project

Linux, Windows-CE, and Android are the most used embedded OS (eOS). Amongst them, Android open-source platform stands out as the most widely utilized. It is developed by the Open Handset Alliance, a group of 71 technology and mobile companies, whose objective is to create a free, mobile software platform. In our system, Kitkat version of Android Platform was adopted.

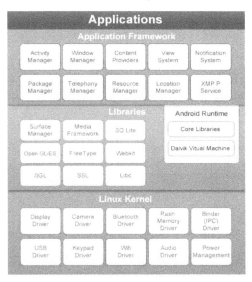

Fig. 3. Android architecture.

The Android platform includes an operating system, middleware and applications. As for the features, Android incorporates the common features found nowadays in any mobile device platform, such as application framework reusing, integrated browser, optimized graphics, media support, and network technologies, etc. The Android architecture, depicted in Figure 3, is composed of five layers: Applications, Application Framework, Libraries, Android Runtime and finally the Linux kernel. The Linux kernel, version 3.0, is the bottommost layer and is also a hardware abstraction layer (HAL) that enables the interaction of the upper layers with the hardware layer via device drivers. Furthermore, it also provides the most fundamental system services such as security, memory management, process management and network stack.

In order to port android on our hardware, we have configured android open source platform, HAL and implemented several device driver code in kernel such as Omnivision cameras (OV3640 and OV5640), LCD, Touchscreen, Battery charger, Power regulator etc.,

C. Zigbee network

Zigbee is a protocol that had been developed based on Open System Interconnection (OSI) layer model. It builds on IEEE standard 802.15.4 which defines the physical and Medium Access Control (MAC) layers. Zigbee supports three types of communication topologies; star topology, tree topology and mesh topology. Zigbee wireless device operates with very-low power consumption which makes it the most attractive wireless device to use in Wireless Sensor Network (WSN). Zigbee has multi-hop communication capability, hence providing an unlimited range of communication. Nowadays, several Zigbee operating systems are being developed by various organizations. We used Z-Stack, developed by Texas Instruments.

D. Patient registration and management system

There are some number of hospitals that are using MIS in their patients' data management processes. These are limited to expensive and immobile systems. On the other hand, the need in Mongolia is to have inexpensive and mobile system that is capable of managing patient's data. Herein, we implemented such an information system that meets the above requirements. It is designed for managing a database of patients who are being treated for hepatitis as it is one of the critical situations that Mongolian medical professionals are faced with.

III. System Implementation

A. Hardware design and implementation

The Altium designer tool was used to design and develop the hardware. In this tablet, we have used Exynos4412 CPU module which has simplified the PCB designing process. Therefore, the base Printed Circuit Board (PCB) of the tablet was designed with 0.8mm thickness, 2 layers and several high speed components or interfaces such as LVDS, USB, HDMI. One attractive advantage of Altium Designer is the possibility of setting special rules on partial connection objects. For example, in tablet's USB data connection, minus and plus data lines must be routed with 95 Ohm differential impedance and their lengths must be matched. Thus, the proposed tablet incorporates several high speed digital interfaces and components that follow standard or predetermined special rules for some parts of PCB.

B. Android porting

The advent of Android has generated tremendous interest in the developer community to customize the same for their products running on other embedded platforms. The android porting implementation is shown in Figure 4. In order to port Android on our tablet, following steps are implemented:

1. Preparing the build environment

Ubuntu 14.04 version is recommended for build environment. On Ubuntu, use OpenJDK and arm-linux-gcc for building Android. The latest version of Android requires Java 7. After installing Java, required packages also must be installed.

2. Porting the bootloader

The Linux kernel makes some fundamental assumption when it gets control from a bootloader. The bootloader mus have initialized the DRAM controller. Linux assumes that th system RAM is present and fully functional. Therefore, th boot loader should also initialize the system memory map This is usually done via a set of processor registers.

3. Porting the Linux kernel

Kernel is loaded in RAM and run by bootloader. T customize Linux kernel into Android, Androidisms must b done on it such as wakelocks, lowmem handler, binder, RAM console, logger etc .,

4. Developing device drivers

Everything in Unix is a file, including devices. Fo developing device drivers, use standard Linux model API, tr avoiding wakelocks in drivers and use modules fo development. We have implemented several device driver such as Omnivision cameras (OV3640 and OV5640), LCD Touchscreen, Battery charger, Power regulator etc.,

5. Implementing Android hardware libs (HAL)

Hardware abstraction layer (HAL), layer between th kernel and the application framework, is very important fo porting Android to a custom board. Especially, whe integrating new devices to a custom board such as inpu sensors.

6. Customizing the user space

Fig. 4. Android porting implementation.

User-space is customized by changing boot screen, statu bar, preloaded applications, themes, adding new application and adding new hardware type.

IV. Experiment

The proposed tablet was implemented in real mode. Th experimental tablet is shown in Figure 5. It has built-i medical purpose android application, which is for patien registration, monitoring, and management. Also this system works with web server based data base, which stores a patient's data.

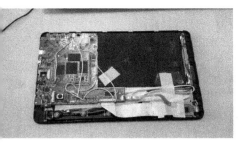

Fig. 5. Implemented Medical Android Tablet featuring Zigbee technology.

The Zigbee network has been tested by communicating blet as the coordinator. Also, other end-node sensors and uters are used for experiment. The experimental network esign of Zigbee featured sensor network and Medical ndroid Tablet is shown in Figure 6.

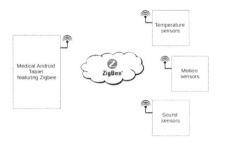

Fig. 6. Experimental network design of Zigbee featured sensor network and edical Android Tablet.

In this work, the experiment was implemented through a esh network between coordinator Tablet, up to 20 sensor odes and routers. We used Zigbee based room temperature nsors, motion sensors, and sound detection sensor for etwork experimental purpose. The outdoor application range as up to 200 meters depending on environment aracteristics and the indoor application range was up to 30 meters depending on the room numbers and environment. After implementing routers, the communication range was extended nearly twice larger.

V. CONCLUSION AND FUTURE WORK

The developed tablet was successfully executed with the help of correlating Zigbee module, Android OS and Exynos 4412 based processor system. The implemented Zigbee module's communication range was within 20 meters indoor and up to 200 meters outdoor. Also, it is possible to extend communication range using routers. In this research work, we used temperature sensors, motion sensors and sound sensors for testing Zigbee network. For future development, we are planning to design and integrate Zigbee based personal healthcare equipments to the system. It will enable nurses to monitor multiple patients in the hospital area and increase medical quality.

Acknowledgment

The research was supported by Ametros Solutions LLC and ONOM foundation grant.

References

[1]   Chien Yu Peng, Wei Shin Kao, You Zhao Liang and Wen Ko Chiou, "The Practices of Scenario Observation Approach in Defining Medical Tablet PC Applications," J. Jacko (Ed.): Human-Computer Interaction, Part IV, HCII 2007, LNCS 4553, pp. 518-524, 2007, Springer-Verlag Berlin Heidelberg 2007

[2]   http://en.wikipedia.org/wiki/Exynos

[3]   Cláudio Maia, Luis Miguel Nogueira, Luis Miguel Pinho, "Evaluating Android OS for Embedded Real-Time Systems", HURRAY-TR-100604, 06-29-2010

[4]   Sung Wook Moon, Young Jin Kim, Ho Jun Myeong, Chang Soo Kim, Nam Ju Cha, and Dong Hwan Kim, "Implementation of Smartphone Environment Remote Control and Monitoring System for Android Operating System-based Robot Platform", 2011 8th International Conference on Ubiquitous Robots and Ambient Intelligence (URAI), Nov. 23-26, 2011 in Songdo ConventiA, Incheon, Korea

[5]   Kalpik M. Patel, Chirag K. Patel, "Porting Android on Arm Based Platform", International Journal of Innovative Research in Computer and Communication Engineering Vol.1, Issue 3, may 2013

[6]   Karim Yaghmour, "Embedded Android" book

[7]   Alessandro Rubini, "Linux Device Drivers" book

[8]   http://free-electrons.com/docs/

[9]   www.opersys.com

Observer Regulation for Energy-Efficient Group-Value Applications

Daniel Reißner, Wolfram Hardt,
Technische Universität Chemnitz, Germany
{daniel.reissner, wolfram.hardt}@informatik.tu-chemnitz.de

Abstract— In order to balance energy in sensor networks, neighbour energy level or rate of delivery have to be observed. Based on observation, importance of energy weight has to be defined for forwarding decision. In other scenario of increasing number of applications, acceptance level has to be adapted in time with increasing arrival rate. In order to process huge amount of data in time, automatization is required, which regulates the preference decision also on higher abstraction level with increasing number of data. In this work an observer architecture is introduced, which organizes the parameter weighting on existing factory related systems in energy efficient way.

Keywords— energy-efficient, preference, group-value, observer-mechanism

I. INTRODUCTION

In order to realize energy efficient routing in factories, routing decisions of nodes have to be selected in an energy efficient way, so that the overall energy of network is balanced. By balancing the network energy, nodes stay active for a long time and the network stays functional until recharge point in time. For extension of routing approaches by consideration of energy an observer approach is appropriate which checks whether to route by current policy e.g. shortest path or by considering the energy reserves. With Observation rules, conditions are applied like minimal neighbour energy difference or number of successful message deliveries.

Influencing factors for production are qualification of users and technological support by measurement instruments.

For acceptance of applicants on university, application requirements have to be checked (Bachelor degree for master study, transferability of courses of other study programs, Certificates and further qualifications). Furthermore all organizational places have to be informed (PDF generation, evaluation, processing and overview documents, contradiction documents). A fast and controlled processing can be supported by an automatic acceptance suggestion. Observation of receiving number of applicants allows for re-regulation of acceptance level in order to accept the allowed number up to maximal allowed number of acceptable students per semester.

Image based measurement devices for determination of chain elongation of industrial chains have to rate pixel structures in a model and regulate with each video data frame.

With increasing complexity of hierarchical data sources and evaluation proceedings, a describing approach is required to describe single cases in a grouped way in order to make them easier to handle and extendable and to define weighting adaptions on the system.

II. STATE OF THE ART

In [1] a evaluation mechanism called preference was introduced based on weights wi. It allowed for routing considering signal quality, energy and hop count. In [2] the preference mechanism was applied to applications for master program ASE of TU Chemnitz in Summer Term 2015. In [3] a flexible data structure "group value format" was introduced which allowed for energy efficient calculation of preference by short messages and direct data access. The direct access extends structs/classes by variable elements without the effort of next pointer of lists and supports, realized in sql-database the processing of data from various sources.

III. CONCEPT

In this work, the preference concept, operating on group value format, was extended by observer layer as state in Fig. 1. The observer represents a meta function on existing system which performs weight adaptions by iterative step width tests and measurements.

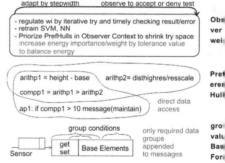

Fig. 1: three layer observer architecture

A corresponding controller, which realizes this architecture, supports the operations set and get parameterized by group conditions. The set operator allows for realization of Insert/Update web forms, which automatically insert new form fields type-based in data base or adds new sensors as attributes in database.

The preference controller optimizes an energy oriented equation of the form:

$$(1) \quad \max f = \max\left(\cfrac{1}{\left[\sum_{path=0}^{t} f(path-1) + (cSendE * Msglen) * rtcnt \atop +twake\right] * ncnt}\right)$$

There, the energy parameters like the pathlenght in a sensor network is considered recursively. Sendpower per message depends on message length and retransmission count and the amount of sensor nodes. Synchronization to production rates allows optimal sleep times without additional energy consumption of wakeup receivers. For higher adaptivity to variable events, thereby, it is possible to use distributed node wake preferences as grouplocal synchronization criterium. In case of indicators for alarm situation, this way an early synchronization optimization is possible. For server applications, number of servers is energy criteria. Hopcount could be reduced by placing function in database in case of server application. Message length of images is reduced by pdf generation, ocr detection, svg and direct form data processing. Organization in user adpted group views extends state graph by on demand group forming on subsets of nodes and edges. User role views save processing time and allow for longer sleep times of low power client computers, which only have to be equipped with browser functionality.

IV. RESULTS

For a task database (for appointments, specifications and online exam tasks Fig. 3 top) a load test with group-value concept of iterative flexible single data access (low data amount, status selects) and index lifting for mass data request was compared with the MySQL join concept. The iterative access allows for faster by instant results without waiting while for join user has to wait until it is completely processed. Indexing of flexible data in the typ relation allows for maximal performance. The join concept allows for low data amounts more bad response times for complete join processing and is inappropriate for big data amounts because big sets have to be traversed and connected. There the generic concept of index lifting of flexible data shows best results Fig. 3 middle. There the load test was also applied for bigger data amounts. Another problem is the incompleteness of left-Join, so that for missing elements in the left relation the values in the right relation are not found. This way group value format is more expressive and allows for selection of attributes if they are available as required. Because of not required table combinations, much more attributes can be traversed completely (fig. 3 bottom) compared to many joins. Group attributes allow jump across areas and object links can be resolved directly or extended by functions.

In order to realize energy balancing in sensor networks, network in Fig. 4 was realized. The energy balancing is activated on hop-preference based network by reaching a tolerance value. Therefore energy values have to be provided to node in seldom (because of slowly decreasing energy) requests. An observer uses the informations for an energy oriented forwarding or to decide forwarding based on shortest path.

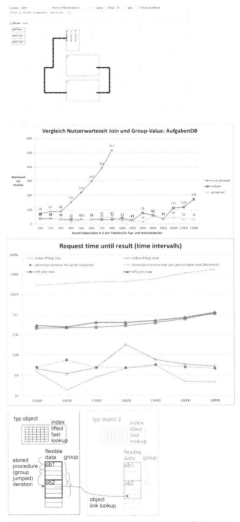

Fig. 3: top: sample Application for online Tasks and Specifications on application database; middle: time in ms for request to task database, for load up to 30000 data objects to firefox output, maximal performance with stored procedure and index lifting; bottom: iterative stored procedure lookup in instance objects following typ object, on demand lookup by group conditions and object links

9

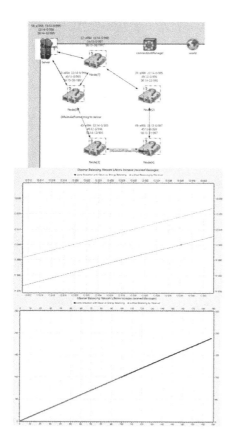

Fig. 4: simulation of observer energy balancing; top: sample network with server target and nodes[3] source; middle: increased latency by observer selected energy efficient longer paths; bottom: result extension of network lifetime by 50% and doubling number of server received messages by better utilizing node resources by observer balancing;

In order to determine the chain elongation of industrial chains (Fig. 5), an observer mechanism was developed, which detects the video frame detected circles as carrier belt circles based on movement vector detection, position update and redetection count. Furthermore it provides distance to base wheel and approximates the arc length. Iterative check of step

with from forming movement vectors is realized by observer based on position update measurements.

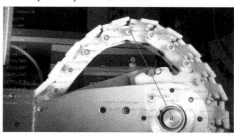

Fig.5. robust detection results by application of Observer control loop using adaptive circle movement vector rates

The application tool for Master ASE was extended by an observer to adapt the evaluation border of accepted students. This evaluation border is iteratively adapted based on current count of applications per semester. The observer realizes a check and movement of set hull.

V. CONCLUSION AND OUTLOOK

In this work an architecture was presented, which allows for description of complex systems by grouping preferences and defining observer-rules on top of it. This allows by a compact group-value format energy-saving short messages. Furthermore, the group-value format allows longer sleep times of system by faster response by combination of iterative stored procedure with index lifting. Hierarchical preference integrations and observer rules allow direct data access (low interface overhead). This way Tools only need browser on client side and routing application can work on low power microcontrollers.

Routing regulation mechanism can be extended by comparison with increase in rate of delivery. Observer mechanism can be used for targeted exploration by introducing an experience based priority context data structure. Therefore extension of preference by situation dependent priorities is required.

REFERENCES

[1] D. Reissner, F. Strakosch, Energy-efficient adaptive communication by preference-based routing and forecasting, *SSD 11-14 Feb. 2014*

[2] Daniel Reißner, Wolfram Hardt, Energieeffizientes Routing auf Basis des Nutzerfortschritts, CE Workshop, April 2015,

[3] Daniel Reißner, Wolfram Hardt "In Process Homogeneous Object-Binding Structure for Preference Zone Based Decision Making", Knowledge-Based Software Engineering 11th Joint Conference JCKBSE 2014, Volgograd Russia, September 17-20, 2014

Future Development of Mobile 5G Technology in Mongolia, Its Network Planning

Otgonbaatar, Yura
Information and Communication Department
Huree University of Information and Communication
Technology
Ulaanbaatar, Mongolia
otgonbaatar@huree.edu.mn

Uranchimeg, Tudevdagva
School of Power Engineering,
Mongolian University of Science and Technology
Ulaanbaatar, Mongolia
uranchimeg@must.edu.mn

Abstract— this paper describes the research idea on development of mobile 5G technology to improve the information and communication technology of Mongolia.
The rapid development of mobile communications, Internet and high-speed broad band transmission systems are determining trend development of global Information and Communication Technology (ICT).
This research work studied and analyzed the global ICT trend and described the current level of Mongolian ICT.
By 2020, mobile generation and advanced technology 5G are being planned for introduction in countries around of the world. As research work, we studied how to optimize the network structure of mobile 5G technology and designed a network management system solution to use this technology in Mongolia.

Keywords— Mobile communication, Mongolian ICT, integrated system, 1G, 2G, 3G, 4G, 5G

I. INTRODUCTION

The growth in telecommunication is very sharp during last little decades.
The main contribution in this growth of industry is wireless mobile communication industry.
The growth of this industry has experienced several generations. These systems have evolved through the first generation (1G) to the fourth generation (4G), with typical services and representative technologies for each generation. For example, 1G is analog cellular system, while the second generation (2G) is digital system based on TDMA or FDMA. Both 1G and 2G are mainly designed for circuit switched voice application.
The third generation (3G) is characterized by CDMA and designed for packet switched services including multi-media. OFDM and MIMO are the key technologies of 4G which supports wideband data and mobile internet services. Recently, with the fast development of the integrated circuit (IC) technology, powerful cellular networks and terminals already exist.
Various wireless communication technologies are converging to provide all types of exciting new services.
It is foreseen that the future 5G cannot be defined by a single type of service or technology.

The 5G wireless communication system will be a converged system with multiple radio access technologies integrated together.
It can support a wide range of applications and services to comprehensively satisfy the requirements of the information society by the year 2020 and beyond. [1]

II. THE LITERATURE REVIEW

From the roots of analog based first generation service 1G - Frequency Division Multiple Access (FDMA) to today`s truly broadband 4G - Orthogonal Frequency Division Multiple Access (OFDMA), the wireless industry is on a path that promises some great innovation in our future.
These generations are 1G, 2G, 3G, and 4G. Each generation have some standards, capacities, techniques and new features which differentiate it from previous generation. [2]

A. The First Generation (1G)-Analog System

The first operational cellular communication system was developed in the Norway in 1981 and was followed by similar in the US and UK. [3].

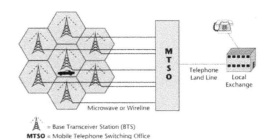

Fig.1 Network architecture of AMPS [4]

These first generation system Advanced Mobile Phone System (AMPS) was provided only voice transmissions by using frequencies around 800-900MHz on based analogue modulated schema FDMA.

AMPS network consisted mobile user, Base Transceiver Station (BTS), and Mobile Telephone Switching Office (MTSO). (Figure 1)

- Poor Voice Quality
- Poor Battery Life
- Large Phone Size
- Limited Capacity

Access FDMA with 30 kHz channels occupying and first commercial cellular system deployed until the early 1990`s [5]

B. The Second Generation (2G)- Digital System

The second generation (2G) wireless mobile system is digital cellular systems.
Comparing with first generations and second generation wireless system used completely digital modulation schema, such as Time Division Multiple Access (TDMA) and Code Division Multiple Access (CDMA). [3]

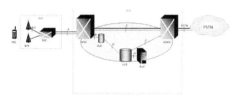

Fig.2 Network architecture of GSM [7]

While Global Systems for Mobile Communication (GSM) technology was developed in Europe (Figure 2), CDMA technology was developed in North America in 1991. [3]

- It was provided voice and SMS
- Data speed in 2G is up to 64Kbps
- It was provided semi global roaming

C. The Second and Half Generation (2.5G)

2.5G systems introduced enhance the data capacity of GSM and mitigation some of its limitation.
2.5G is used to describe 2G systems that have implemented a packet switched domain in addition to the circuit switched domain. (Figure 3)

- Send and receive E-mail, MMS-(multimedia message)
- Web browsing
- Speed: 64-144 kbps
- Camera phones

General Packet Radio Service (GPRS) could provide data rates from 56 Kbit/s up to 115 Kbit/s. It can be used for

service such as Wireless Application Protocol (WAP) access Multimedia Messaging Service (MMS), and for Internet communication services such as email and World Wide Web access. [6]

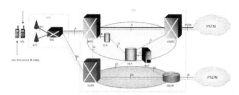

Fig.3 Network architecture of GPRS [7]

GPRS defines how to add IP support to the existing GSM architecture.

D. The Third Generation (3G)- Internet System

The goal of 3G wireless system was to provide wireless data service with data rates of 144kbps to 384 kbps in wide coverage areas, and 2Mbps in local coverage areas.

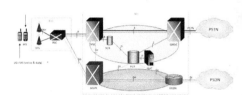

Fig.4 Network architecture of 3G [7]

The 3G architecture is required to provide a greater level of performance to that of the original GSM network. (Figure 4)

- It was provided voice, data, video
- Send/Receive large Email Message
- High Speed Web
- Video Conferencing and 3D Gaming
- TV Streaming, Mobile TV

3rd generation mobile system was adopted by Japan and South Korea in 2001 for the first time. [2]

E. The Fourth Generation (4G)- Integrated System

4G refers to ALL-IP packet switched networks, mobile ultra-broadband (from 100Mbs to 1Gbps speed) access and multi-carrier transmission. (Figure 5)
The technologies under the 4G umbrella are: Long Term Evolution (LTE) and Worldwide Interoperability for Microwave Access (Wi-MAX). [2]
Both technologies are technically very similar in their ways of transmitting signals and rates. Both LTE and WiMAX use Multiple Input Multiple Output MIMO that the information i

nt to two or more cell phones antennas in order to improve ception.

oth systems also use OFDMA, a technology that supports reaming video and Multimedia.

FDMA is a mature and highly proven technology that works y separating the signal into multiple frequencies narrow, with ts of data sent at the same time [8].

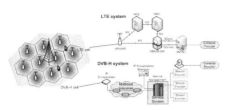

Fig.5 Network architecture of 4G

ne of the basic terms used to describe 4G is MAGIC:

- **M**obile Multimedia
- **A**nytime Anywhere
- **G**lobal Mobility Support
- **I**ntegrated Wireless Solution
- **C**ustomized Personal Service

TE will support mixed data, voice, video and messaging affic and multimedia services.

III. THE FUTURE FIFTH MOBILE GENERATION-(5G)

Currently 5G is not a term officially used in any official GPP, WiMAX Forum or ITU-R. [6]

lthough, ITU approved the first release of the 4G global re standard (GCS) In January 2012.

fter the world radio communication conferences 2012 WRC-12), telecommunication industry began to discuss the sions and requirements of 5G.

This section provides views on the 5G vision from several erspectives, including social perspective, user's perspective nd operator's perspective. Based on the visions, key quirements of 5G are also proposed. [1]

The 5G vision from social perspective

5G is expected to play even a larger role in the year 2020 nd beyond, and its social responsibilities and functions can be ummarized as following four aspects.

- Wireless information circulation system of human ecosystems
- Ubiquitous Connectivity
- Information centre of people's life
- Infrastructure for variety of fundamental communication services

B. The 5G vision from user's perspective

In the era of 5G, mobile system will enhance user's experience in many aspects such as: higher demand, good performance, easy to use, affordable, safety and reliability, and personalization.

C. The 5G vision from user's perspective

For an operator, diversified applications and sustained revenue growth are the key points of interest in the 5G network. Following aspects are important for sustainable growth.

- Sufficient bandwidth and capacity
- Low cost and easy to deploy
- Service diversification and increasing revenue
- Backward compatibility and investment protection

D. Technical requarments of 5G

Based on above analysis of the 5G vision from several perspectives, preliminary technical requirements of the 5G (Figure 6)

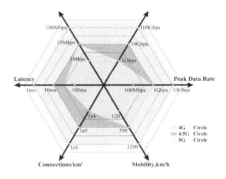

Fig.6 Key capabilities of 5G [1]

5G are given below:

- X1000 mobile data traffic compared to current traffic volume, for example, more than 100Gbps/km2 throughput,
- X100 connections, for example, more than 1million connections/km2,
- 10Gbps peak data rate,
- Above 10Mbps affordable per user data rate anywhere and anytime, and 100Mbps for some special users,
- Lower latency, delay in milliseconds (ms) for end-to-end user plane, and within 10ms for control plane, - higher spectrum efficiency, 3-5 times higher than

today for large area coverage and even higher for special cases,

- Lower cost, nearly 1/1000 of cost per bit than today,
- Higher energy efficiency, nearly 1/1000 of energy consumption per bit than today.

The 5G objectives such as x1000 current mobile data traffic, x100 current connected devices, 10Mbps - 100Mbps user data rate experience anywhere and anytime and etc, need to be met with limited frequency bandwidth.

Besides, increasing frequency allocation and spectrum efficiency, considering more popular scenarios of indoor and hotspot for future data traffic, ultra dense network tends to be one of the most promising technical solutions, however, interference coordination and network planning and optimization will be challenging. [1]

Comparison study of mobile generation has been shown by scientist researchers in some science paper. (Table1)

TABLE 1

1G	2G/2.5G	3G	4G	5G
1980	1990	2000	2010	2020
Multiplexing				
FDMA	TDMA CDMA	CDMA	CDMA	CDMA
Switching				
Circuit	Circuit	Circuit/ Packet	Packet	All packet
Technology				
Analog	Digital	Broadband	Ultra broadband	4G+WWWW
Core network				
PSTN	PSTN Packet	Packet network	Internet	Internet
Data rate				
2kbps	64-144kbps	2mbps	100mbps to 1gbps	>1gbps
Services				
Voice	Voice, SMS, Data	Voice, Data, Audio, Video	Multimedia	Integrated
Handoff				
Horizontal	Horizontal	Horizontal	Horizontal & Vertical	Horizontal & Vertical

Comparison of mobile generation

5G is to be a new technology that will provide all the possible applications, by using one universal device, and interconnecting most of the already existing communication infrastructures.

The goal of 5G is complete wireless communication system having no limitation and is called as *Real World Wireless* or *World Wide Wireless Web* (WWWW). [5]

IV. MOBILE COMMUNICATION AND SERVICE IN MONGOLIA

Information and communication sector development is defined by average statistics of per 100 capita, a method by International Telecommunication Union (ITU).

By the 2014 statistics revealed by ITU, there are: [9]

- In developed countries 120 mobile phones, 40 fix phones, 77 internet services per 100 capita.
- In developing countries 90 mobile phones, 11 fix phones, 40 internet services per 100 capita.
- In the world average, there are 95 mobile phones, fixed phones, 31 internet services per 100 capita. [9

A. Some facts of ICT in Mongolia

Mobile service in Mongolia: A mobile service per 1 capita equals 160, which is higher than developed countri This statistical indicator shows that to reach develop countries' level can be done via mobile subscribers. [10]

Internet service in Mongolia: Number of internet servi subscribers has been increased above 200,000 above t previous 3 years and per 100 capita equals 66.

At this rate of increase, Mongolia will reach the sar level as developed countries in the very near future. [10]

B. Mobile service in Mongolia

Mongolia has 4 mobile operator companies: Mobico Skytel, Unitel and G-Mobile with total subscribers 4,971,719 by the 2014. (Table 2)

TABLE II

Mobile Operators	Technology	Subscriber	Coverage
Mobicom	GSM-2G, 3.5G	1,860,381	301
Skytel	2G-CDMA, 3.75G	678,317	232
Unitel	GSM-2G, 3.5G	1,247,474	269
G-Mobile	2G-CDMA,3G	460,847	261
Total		4,971,719	1103

Compared characteristic of mobile compan

All mobile network operators have introduced 3G (Thi Generation), 3,5G technology services [11].

Mongolia is a special country because much of population is centralized in Ulaanbaatar. Outside the capi city and population density is low with vast unpopulated are and a nomadic culture.

Communications Regulatory Commission of Mongolia planning to announce new licenses for mobile operat companies for the purpose of introducing 4G technology 2016.

Mobile operator companies are currently using 3G, 3.5 technologies. Therefore upgrades to software and hardwa are necessary to fully support a mobile 4G network.

Therefore, the purpose of our research was to study t optimization of network structure of 5G technologies a design a network management solution before the 5 technology is introduced in Mongolia.

V. RESEARCH APPROACH AND METHODS

In our research, we studied how to optimize t network structure of mobile 5G technology and designed network management system solution in preparation for t arrival of technology in Mongolia.

Therefore, we offer some solutions to develop networks with 5G technology.

Possible Network solution 1

There are 381 soums, 23 provinces, and the capital city of Ulaanbaatar located in Mongolia [12].
Currently, a mobile network solution is non optimal for an ICT network.
In Mongolia, all mobile operator companies have installed their own BTS (Base Station Transceiver) in the center of aimags and all soums to connect via separate networks. (Figure 7)

Fig. 7 Development of 5G network in soun of Mongolia

The result is four BTS of each operator is working in population markets.
Therefore only one BTS (Base Transceiver Station) of 5G network should be installed by one mobile operator to support sparsely populated area.
We have calculated [theoretically] to define capacity, coverage and technical parameters that needed to install a base station in each soum.
We have calculated to define coverage it is included: macro BTS, its radius 15km. (1)

$$S = \pi r^2 = 3.14 * (15_{km})^2 = 700 km^2 \quad (1)$$

As calculated that 30 users in square, it is approximately 21000 users in coverage cell of base station. (2)
Average soum population is 5000-10000.

$$N_{total} = 30_{user} * S = 21000_{us} \quad (2)$$

According to these calculations, it is possible to install one base station in a soum via capacity of subscriber, traffic call and coverage. (1), (2)
Subscribers of another operator company can use local roaming service to connect to other operator networks to make calls.

Possible Network solution 2

Currently, the mobile basic network is organized by centralized structure network solutions.
All mobile operator companies have installed a mobile switching center in the capital city Ulaanbaatar wich is connected to networks installed BTS in the center of provinces and soums. This is a non optimal solution for technical reliability because if there are any technical problems the central mobile switching center will not connect to all networks.
Therefore, Mongolian provinces must be divided according to geographical regionally with a ring connection fiber optic backbone by on based DWDM.

Fig. 8 Development of 5G network in province of Mongolia

DWDM can be used to create separated structure networks within the main mobile communication network. (Figure 8)

Possible Network solution 3

If we develop Mobile communication 5G network in Ulaanbaatar, it will be used hexagonal structure cell design and more developed method of cell splitting.

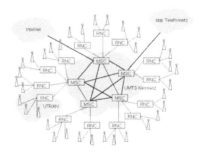

Fig. 9 Development of 5G network in Ulaanbaatar

It should be built connection fiber optic backbone network by MESH topology among Mobile Switching Centers of operator companies; Mobicom, Unitel, Skytel, and G-Mobile. (Fig 9)

CONCULISION

In this research, we defined the trend of global information, defined communications, and statistics indicators and presented the evolution of cellular mobile communications, innovation and development of the future in mobile communication.

Finally as research work, we studied how to optimize the network structure of mobile 5G technology and designed a network management system solution in preparation for using this technology in Mongolia

In the future: Mongolia's population is around 3,000,000 with the population of mobile units in use at 4,971,719 [2014]. Some subscribers are using mobile phones from each operator companies.

Their reason is quality of service, tariffs, different promotions, network coverage, advantages of technology and number of choices. When compared to our population, Mongolia has a large traffic volume in its ICT communication networks.

If 5G technology can replace existing ICT networks system, then the number of mobile units will be reduced by 50%.

Therefore, Mongolia should develop: machine to machine (M2M), technology to technology (T2T) and device to device (D2D) of 5G.

References

[1]   Evolution, Convergence, and Innovation 5G white paper, Datang Wireless Mobile Innovation Center, December, 2013

[2]   Engr. Muhammad Farooq, Engr. Muhammad Ishtiaq Ahmed, Engr Usman M AI: Future Generations of Mobile Communication Networks Academy of Contemporary Research Journal-2013 /P.24-P.29/

[3]   Vasco Pereira and Tiago Sousa: Evolution Mobile Communication from 1G to 4G, Voice Calls to Ubiquitous Multimedia Group Communication

[4]   Codeidol.com: 1G: Analog Transmission

[5]   Xichun Li, Abudulla Gani, Rosli Salleh, Omar Zakaria: The Future of Mobile Wireless Communiation Networks, 2009 International Conference on Communication Software and Networks

[6]   Mudit Ratana Bhalla, Anand Vardhan Bhalla: Generations of Mobile Wireless Technology: A Survey, International Journal of Computer Application (August 2010), P26-P30

[7]   Amrul.tumblr.com: Mobile Network Evolution: GSM to UMTS

[8]   Zeendo.com: 4G Mobile generation; LTE and WiMAX

[9]   www.itu.int, Global Mobile Statistics 2014 Part A: Mobile subscribers handset market share, mobile operators

[10] crc.gov.mn: Main indicators of telecommunications sector end of 2014

[11] Mobicom.mn, Skytel.mn, Unitel.mn, G-Mobile.mn

[12] Mongolian Yearbook-2014

[13] Otgonbaatar. Yu; Buyankhishig. Z: "Some possibility of E-integrated network solution" Proceeding of International Summer workshop Computer Science-2013 /page 32-35/ Jul. 2013. (Chemnitz, Germany)

[14] Otgonbaatar. Yu; Buyankhishig. Z : "Information and Communication Technology: Some possibility to develop through solution of integrated network in other sectors of Mongolia" IFOST-2013 Proceedings of "The 8th International Forum on Strategic Technology 2013" /page 310-313/ Jul.2013. (Ulaanbaatar, Mongolia)

The Automatic Diagnostic by Pulse Based on the Expert System

Yumchmaa Ayush
Faculty of Automation and Computer
Engineering
Novosibirsk State Technical University
Novosibirsk, Russia
Power Engineering School
Mongolian University of Science and
Technology
Ulaanbaatar, Mongolia
yumchmaa@must.edu.mn

Grif M.G
Faculty of Automation and
Computer Engineering
Novosibirsk State Technical
University
Novosibirsk, Russia
grifmg@mail.ru

Uranchimeg Tudevdagva
Power Engineering School
Mongolian University of Science and
Technology
Ulaanbaatar, Mongolia
uranchimeg@must.edu.mn

Abstract – **The pulse is still one of the most important diagnostic. This paper deals with theoretical idea on basic elements of pulse diagnosis is provided to illuminate progresses in its study using computational methods. Recent time, the traditional diagnosis and treatment is often used in modern medicine, in particular those on pulse diagnosis. Traditional medical classics provide graphic descriptions of the various types of pulses to be recognized.**

The rapid development of computational technology opens many opportunities to use such expert systems in public services in particular of health. The use of medical diagnostic expert system in medical is essential. Most medical expert systems designed for diagnosis, to give advice about drug treatment for disease and rehabilitation services. These are has been used modern diagnosis knowledge data, that give the response by patient presenting own symptoms in body established in accordance with questions. This paper discusses the use of both modern and traditional medicine is used in the diagnosis of pulse diagnostic method supporting by medical expert systems which is will introduce in information technology.

Keywords—diagnosis; pulse diagnosis; expert system.

I. INTRODUCTION

Healthcare problem is one of the most important sectors in each country. In this sense, researchers have focused implementation any new advanced scientific and technical achievements in use of the healthcare.

First medical expert system for medicine was designed over 40 years ago [1]. From this time, artificial intelligence for search has been developing in the theory used in expert system is database, knowledge base and problem solving. These technical and technological aspects give a chance to researchers for to develop expert systems in medicine. Such expert systems are uses as assistant tools for making decision to medical specialists.

In the middle of 1970, four experimental systems are regarded as having started the research field artificial intelligence in medicine. These are MYCIN, PROSPECTOR, CASNET, PIP [2]. All four drew on artificial intelligence techniques, emphasizing the encoding of large amounts of specialized medical knowledge acquired from the clinical literature and from expert collaborators. One of these four experimental systems is namely MYCIN, to advise physicians on antibacterial selection for patients with bacteremia or meningitis. As well as similar expert systems are named ONCOCIN, DIAVAL, DENDRAL, PUFF, HERSAY-II, that had been using in medicine [3,4].

Expert system for medicine developed usually for physician, nurse or for procedure of healthcare. Expert system for patient is at the first patient entering information about health situation then will be explain what kind of medical problem detected in body. If patient requires confirmation, expert system explains to patient based on facts and evidence how comes to such decision. Expert system for medical personnel (doctors, nurses, etc.) designed as a diagnosing or treatment consultation [5]. Concept to treat human is not only theory who taught in the university. Doctors have own features of the experience and feelings. Such many external factors estimate management of patient treatment and patient's situation of diseases. In the sense, expert system based on the knowledge of experiment has a probability to make a same decision with young doctors. Development of information technology gives opportunity to improve state of this theory. It increases a requirement to generate self-diagnostic system and to get a new level [15].

Recent time, modern medicine is focusing to one big conception that to teach early prevent illness and probable diseases identify source properly. It helps to earlier diagnosis any diseases and rapidly decides how it treats too. Under this idea, in front of researchers have a big issue to facilitate kind of diagnosing process without physician, it is will assist any patients can diagnosis yourself and will enable to delicacy treatment for diseases early. Medical expert system is based on fundamental medical knowledge, problem solving process and management to patient.

II. MODERN AND TRADITIONAL PULSE DIAGNOSTICS METHODLOGIES

Nowadays global trend is envisioned as enabling investigation to identify base of any decease not only based on the standard method and parameters. This means to use development of information technology for a medicine and to increase opportunities of multi-diagnosing process. Specially, worlds' most researchers working intensively how to use artificial intelligence programming and smart algorithm as well as discrete technology, which using measurement method traditional treatment and diagnosing method, pulse diagnosis (diagnosis by palpation) or western medical method is analysis. If this aim is reached successfully, it will lead to virtual modern medical diagnosing equipment based not only theoretical and applied method [6].

For example, automated diagnostic systems can be built by pulse diagnostic method that combines artificial intelligence. Pulse diagnosis has been used in both of modern and traditional medicine [7]. The modern diagnostic process is constructed on correlation of separate pathological signs (disease symptoms) with various anatomic bodies and fabrics (and also with data of laboratory analyses) — on the basis of the model of development of this or that disease accepted in medical science in the form of selection of "nosological units"[8]. For the analysis of pulse attracts the mathematical apparatus for signal processing and for measurement of signals uses an electrode, the transducer and sensors to clarify controlling and diagnosing human cardiovascular system [9].

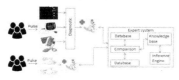

Figure 1. Structure of self-diagnostic system by pulse

In Tibetan medicine diagnosis is divided into three sections [6, 9]:

- Visual observation
- Touch
- Questioning

Diagnosis through touch in Tibetan medicine is performed by pulse reading. The pulse gives to physician specially information about patient [11]. It diagnostic method is only based on the experience and feeling of physicians. In this method not used any measurement techniques. Pulse diagnostic refers along with the different qualities and speed of the pulse. It helps to diagnosis so many diseases further all of organs situation [12]. This knowledge base will be automated using combination of modern and traditional methods of pulse diagnosis gives an opportunity to diagnose a various diseases.

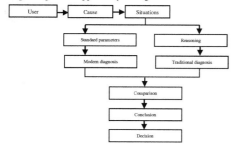

Figure 2. Schematic diagram of diagnostic system

When using a method of pulse diagnostics of tradition medicine the analysis of the diagnostic importance o temporary parameters pulse a signal of a beam artery fc definition of a condition of regulatory systems of an organism was carried out. Studying of the diagnostic importance o temporary parameters of a pulse signal of a beam artery i relation to a problem of definition of a condition of regulator, systems of the organism diagnosed by tradition of the Tibetan medicine was an objective of this research. The conducted researches are continuation of the works which are conducte in the Buryat scientific center of the Siberian Branch of the Russian Academy of Science since 1983. The source stud base of researches is so far defined and created, pulse sensor are developed and approved, the pilot sample of the diagnosti complex automated pulse is created, work on creation of th expert diagnostic systems realizing two methods of th Tibetan-Mongolian medicine – survey and poll are begun Researches in the field of mathematical processing of pulse signals, creations of covers of expert systems proceed [19].

III. SELF-DIAGNOSTIC SYSTEM BY PULSE TECHNIQUE

Tibetan medicine is one of the ancient medical systems, and i has been in use for over many thousand years. This medicin based on the philosophy of Buddhism and physiology [13] The Normal pulse is a sensitive and precise measurabl standard of health. It enables us to detect early deviations from health. It provides us with a preventive medicine. All of these capabilities are almost completely lacking in our moderr health care system [14]. Blood is constant parameter of the liv organism system. Health human body always changes durin his whole life. Therefore, changes of blood show pathologica differences in human body. However, number of puls diagnostic experiment is limited. As a result, self-diagnosti system by pulse is crucial to development of programming ca expand the scope of application this method. Medical exper system is complex of human machine system. This system makes decision based on the medical knowledge, reasoning explanation and conclusions. An expert system versus softwar with database is included into architecture not only database also include knowledge base of experiments and database fo making rules [16].

Medical expert system consist database, inference engine knowledge base and problem-solving. Version of self diagnostic system by pulse, that including diagnostic method for eastern and western medicine you can see Figure 1. In here future system will work at two basic modes. First mode is wil work to use some measurement techniques and second mode i will work to experience of pulse diagnostic experiment. And information is suggest to medical expert system then will mak a decision.

In the sediagnostic system by pulse will give to comparing, diagnostic practice new methods and techniques integrate in emselves ideas eastern and western medicine. Example of hematic diagram of diagnostic system you can see in Figure New diagnostic system's major objective is being basic andard data of patients' pulse palpation. And, general inciple is being used to suggest diagnosis from both of astern and western medical diagnosis methods.

Figure 3. Application of self-diagnostic system by pulse

Pulse diagnosis method in the traditional medicine ill be useful to develop same diagnosis with modern medical agnosis for cardiovascular system and investigate internal tuation of disease, automatically detect the causal situation 8].

utomated diagnostic format increase the probability of agnosis if disease as well as cause of pulse diagnosis xplained completely will resolve main reason for disease and identify influence other causes of adoptive diseases. Thus, ecessity to create one more database including modern edicine is based on standard parameters which database cluding symptoms of disease, in addition traditional pulse agnosis attributing basic knowledge. So, it will give to pportunity advanced version for solving decision that aking comparison the information delivered from patient etween modern and traditional medicine. Although, we used eneral structure of other researchers' diagnostic expert stems, but advantages of this type of diagnostic expert stem has a user interface relates among user and system. he main purpose of this study to provide correct user terface as well as will introduce hospital that treat using aditional diagnosing method. In addition, this expert system ill be able to use various training (see Figure 3). Using this xpert system for training, it is useful to do practice for udents which study in medical university further young ysicians and medical professionals.

he expert system is different to the other program, including e following properties [17]:

- Something of science knowledge is not simulated, but simulating the activities of the human brain. It has main characteristics the expert systems to distinguish of mathematical formulation.

- Program is further of simple operating logic in addition to reasonable estimate, which is based on knowledge.

- The basic issues are more used than fixed smart algorithms that heuristic approach.

- The advantage of this method is not required defined information and result is highly of probability.

IV. EXPECTED RESULTS

By our research work, we will generate fully automated system based on both of modern and traditional pulse diagnosis method. Furthermore, this system is fully satisfied with the human machine system is supported by the technical parts, that the user interface will design easy to use patient. The system will be developed by theoretical simulations and laboratory collaborations. It is also of high priority to reach into collaboration agreement in area of knowledge base development, information exchange and data sharing to facilitate exchange of information within medical experiments.

Plans for our study as follows:

- To create newly diagnostic expert system based on the same structure of the expert systems.

- To create knowledge base with modern and traditional pulse diagnosis.

- To develop to interconnection among modern and traditional diagnosis.

- To create virtual base of expert's experience.

- To create knowledge base on the signs of diseases diagnosing by pulse that evaluate patient's status.

- To increase probability to introduce in using expert diagnostic system by pulse.

- To increase application to prevent from disease that using expert diagnostic system by pulse etc.

CONCLUSION

The expert systems are one of biggest research field in computer science.

Main newly side of our study is idea to introduce in application diagnostic expert system using by modern and traditional pulse diagnosis methods. Thus, we are considering it helps to reduce the time for diagnosis, increase diagnostic confidence probability and early diagnosis of disease, so, we believe that this system can be used in various training. Efficiency of computer technology was high, cost is reducing. It helps to increase the amount of data and knowledge, and gives to big opportunity to choose smart algorithm to making decisions. Further, we are concluding to join experts of modern and traditional pulse diagnosis method for investigation about this self-diagnostic system by pulse with expert system. The paper presents the use of medical expert systems and illustrates modern and traditional pulse diagnosis such as it application areas.

Now, we are investigating materials about other same expert systems and results of investigation on Russian, English and Mongolian languages further translated materials from Tibetan and other languages.

[1] J.E. Bourne. "Biomedical Engineering Handbook," in Plastics, 2nd ed., vol. 3. J. Peters, Ed. New York: McGraw-Hill, 1964, pp.15-67.

[2] Kulani Makhubele. "Literature Synthesis:Knowledge-Based Expert Systems for Medical Advice Provision", Knowledge-Based Expert Systems, vol. 33, pp. 56-99, Jan. 1979.

[3] Buchanan, Shortliffe. "Rule-based Expert Systems", Belmont, CA: Wadsworth, 1993, pp. 123-135.

[4] D.I.Muromtsev, "Introduction to expert systems technology", [On-line], 93(23). Available: http://www.insycom.ru/html/metodmat/pz/ExpertSystems.pdf [2005].

[5] N.V.Abramov, N.V.Motovilov, N.D.Naumov, S.N.Cherkasov, "Information systems in Medicine", Nizhnevartovsk state humanities university, Russia, 2006, pp.141-145. (in Russian)

[6] T.Uranchimeg, S.Uyanga and A.Yumchmaa "A Prototype of Expert System for Rural Medical Centers", 7th International Conference on Frontiers of Information Technology, Applications and Tools, and the 4th PT-ERC International Symposium on Personalized Medicine (FITAT/ISPM 2014), IEEE Computer Society, July 29 – August 1, 2014, Chang Mai, Thailand. pp.23-26. ISSN: 2288-9973.

[7] L.Kh.Garkavy, N.Yu.Mikhailov, G.N.Tolmachev, A.I.Shikhlyarov, E.P.Vereskunova, "Hardware-software complex of pulse diagnostics for determination adaptive response", Electronic journal, <<Investigated in Russia>>, 2003, pp.2292-2303. (in Russian)

[8] V.A.Linde, "Pulse diagnosis", Center of Homeopathy, St-Petersburg, Russia, 2006. (in Russian)

[9] L.V.Ilyasov, "Biomedical measurement techniques", Undergradu school, Moscow, Russia, 2007, pp.342 (in Russian)

[10] Willis J.Tompkins, John G.Webster, eds., "Design of Microcompu Based Medical Intsrumentation", Peace, Moscow, Russia, 1983, pp.3 385. (in Russian)

[11] Kh.Tumbaa, "The Four medical fundamentals", Official Pr Ulaanbaatar, Mongolia,1991, pp.21-22. /6/ (in Mongolian)

[12] V.V.Boronoev, "The Phycial basic of Pulse diagnosis in Tibe Medicine" autoreferat, Sc.D. Ulan-Ude, Russia, 1999, pp.250. (in Russia

[13] Pasang Y.Arya. "Theory and Teaching. Tibetan Medicin Available:www.tibetanmedicine-edu.org. [2012].

[14] Leon Hammer, "Contemporary Pulse Diagnosis: Introduction to Evolving Method for Learning an Ancient Art- Part 1", Ameri Journal of Acupuncture, Vol. 21, No. 2, 1993, pp.1-16.

[15] Edward H.Shortliffe, "Medical Expert Systems-Knowledge Tools Physicians ", Medical Informatics, Stanford, California, USA, 19 pp.830-839.

[16] T.Uranchimeg, A.Yumchmaa, "An expert systems for med engineering", Proceedings of <<The 8th International Forum on Strate Technology 2013>>, Ulaanbaatar, Mongolia, 2013, pp.515-519.

[17] A.Yumchmaa, R.Davaasuren, "Object Oriented Medical Techn Expert System", International Summerschool Computer Science 20 Proceedings of Summerschool 7-13.July, German, 2014, pp.44-47.

[18] Ch.Ts.Tsidipov, "Pulse diagnosis in Tibetan Medicine", Scier Novosibirsk, Russia, 1988, pp.18-32. (in Russian)

[19] http://ipms.bscnet.ru/labs/lvdjs/resultats.html

Aspects of Computer Sign Language Interpretation System Development

Yuliya S. Manueva
The department of Automated Control System
Novosibirsk State Technical University
Novosibirsk, Russia
E-mail: juleno4eknot1@rambler.ru

Abstract—the paper is focused on semantic analysis software unit development of Russian Language in the computer sign language interpretation system. To define the main demands of future semantic unit historical aspects of computer translation systems elaboration were analyzed. It was determined the necessity of applying the semantic analysis in computer Sign language interpretation system. The aim of the research is modelling the meanings of words in the sentences. The objective of this paper is the implementation of the semantic analysis as one of the most effective ways to solve the problem of homonyms. This work is important, because currently in Russia the problem of communication between the company and deaf people are not fully solved, as there is no system of translation from Russian to Russian sign language and vice versa.

Keywords—computer interpretation system, Sign language, semantic analysis, classifier predicates, homonyms, virtual person

I. INTRODUCTION

In Russia, many adults with hearing disabilities have difficulty of communication with other persons. Sign language is a way of interaction between deaf people. Computer animation of Russian Sign Language can simplify the access of these persons to different information, communication services and other services with which they face every day. There are a lot of interpreter system to help deaf people. In follow chapter several systems are analyzed and their advantages and disadvantages are identified. Software unit developed in a basis of these recommendations is described [1].

II. HISTORICAL ASPECTS OF COMPUTER SIGN LANGUAGE INTERPRETATION SYSTEMS DEVELOPMENT

A. Zardoz System

Computer Sign Language Interpretation systems are considered and comparative analysis is carried out. Zardoz system is a translation system from English to American Sign Language using Interlingua. As a basis of Zardoz system is taken a modular system that works in a specific structure being a frame-based structure. The system architecture is shown in Figure 1.

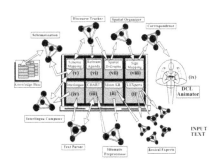

Fig. 1. System Architecture Zardoz

Today, system infrastructure Zardoz is embedded, including analysis, Interlingua, generation and animation components, but it is necessary to implement a comprehensive grammar and vocabulary [2].

B. TEAM System

System TEAM is the first 3D animation system of machine translation from English to American Sign Language, which takes into account not only the linguistic information, but also visual and spatial information related with Sign language. This system shows the specificity of Sign language. This system may be call universal, so it is possible to implement it to other languages. However, the semantic component of language is ignored by the system. To display American Sign language sentences elaborate 3D human model is necessary [3]. This 3D human model is shown in Figure 2.

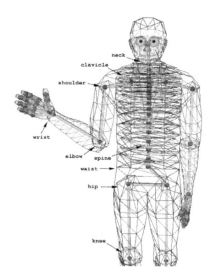

Fig. 2. TEAM Human model

C. ViSiCAST System

ViSiCAST project aims to meet the needs of people with hearing disabilities. In addition to broadcast subtitles, the system is innovative in the field of recognition of a limited range of gestures that allow people with disabilities to communicate with hearing in a social context, such as post offices [4]. Model of human ViSiCAST is presented in Figure 3.

Fig. 3. ViSiCAST Human model

D. Comparative Analysis of Systems

None of the foreign systems can not process the input information received in the voice form. For transfer system, which is directed on interpretation, this lack is significant. Sign languages differ from sounding languages in that deaf people use spatial information about the speaker. Consequently, these systems must take into account the specificity of sign language. Specificity of gesture play is considered only in the Team system. For a more high-quality translation is not sufficient to the morphological and syntactic information. The system attempts to Zardoz account semantic component of sign language. Technology of transfers in ViSiCAST system includes human involvement in the translation process, which is a major disadvantage of this system. All systems displays gestures using the avatar, but only in the ViSiCAST reached the maximum realism.

III. RECOMMENDATION FOR COMPUTER SIGN LANGUAGE INTERPRETATION SYSTEM

Accounting semantic component in the translation process is a great advantage of having such a property. The quality of translation considerably enhanced by this improvement. For best results, you must consider the semantics of the source language and target language. Two systems were considered: Dialing and American Sign Language translation system. For example, these systems can generate recommendations for the development of sign language with the semantic component [5].

Conditionally required model should consist of two parts: the first part is a semantics-sounding language, and the second part reflects the specific Sign language. The main purpose semantic model sounding language lies in resolving the problem of homonyms. For natural translation must take into account classifier predicates. Based on the model, representing classifier predicates in the American system of translation is required to develop a similar system for the Russian language [6]. Accounting voiced demands will lead to higher quality and natural translation, it is understood their target audience – people with disabilities by ear.

IV. SEMANTIC ANALYSIS SOFTWARE UNIT DEVELOPMENT OF RUSSIAN LANGUAGE IN THE COMPUTER SIGN LANGUAGE INTERPRETATION SYSTEM

To define the main demands of future semantic unit historical aspects of computer translation systems elaboration were analyzed. It was determined the necessity of applying the semantic analysis in computer Sign language interpretation system. The aim of semantic analysis software unit development is modelling the meanings of words in the sentences. The objective of this research work is the implementation of the semantic analysis as one of the most effective ways to solve the problem of homonyms. Software module to execute semantic analysis is created with use semantic dictionary database. In this dictionary every word is presented as a set of semantic description. Software unit to execute semantic analysis is shown in Figure 4.

Fig. 4. Software unit

The result of module working is correspondence 'word-gesture". For match making "word-gesture" lexical meanings of words is found. Among quantity of word alternatives on base of semantic analyzer every word in sentence is corresponded only one lexical meaning. Every lexical meaning defines gesture. Recent studies has focused on increase the quantity of gesture and improvement of sentence processing. To achieve first purpose three methods were found. Firstly, to increase the quantity of gesture synonyms are used. It help to translate more Russian words to gestures. Another method is usage antonyms with denial. Short description of words is last methods to increase the database. Today complex sentences are analyzed. Structure of these sentences consists of addition of complex participle construction and analysis of adverb was taken into account.

V. Conclusion

As a result of analysis of the systems their advantages and disadvantages have been identified. The synchronic aspect of presented problem was considered. The main disadvantage of the systems considered is the lack of consideration of the semantic component of both sound language and sign language. It was proved, that accounting semantic component in the translation process is a great advantage of system having this property. The quality of translation considerably enhanced by this improvement. For best results, it must consider the semantics of the source language and target language. To increase the quality of sign language interpreter software unit was developed.

REFERENCES

[1] Grif M.G., Manueva J.S., Kozlov A.N. Development of computer interpretation system - Postroinie sistemi kompiuternogo surdo-perevoda. SPIIRAS Proceedings - Trudy SPIIRAN –, 2014, no. 6 (37), pp. 170–183.

[2] Veale T., Conway A. Cross modal comprehension in ZARDOZ an English to sign-language translation system. Trinity College, 1994. 326 p.

[3] Zhao L., Kipper K., Schuler W. A Machine Translation System from English to American Sign Language. Lecture Notes in Computer Science, 2000, vol. 1934, pp. 54-67.

[4] Wakefield M. VisiCAST. Milestone: Final Report, 2002. 97 p.

[5] Grif M.G., Timofeeva M. K. The problem of automation of sign language from the perspective of applied linguistics - Problemi avtomatizacii surdoperevoda s pozicii prikladnoi lingvistiki. Siberian Journal of Philology Sibirckii filologiskii gurnal, 2012, no.1, pp. 211-219.

[6] M.G.Grif, J.S.Manueva Historical aspects of computer interpretation system to sign language – Istoricheskie aspecti rasvitiya sistem komputernogo surdoperevoda. NSTU Proceedings – Sbornik nauchyh trudov NGTU, in press.

Sensor Integration in Multi-Channel Measurement System Based on The Inverse or The Wiener Filter

Julia S. Petrova, Alexander A. Spector
Dept. of Theoretical Foundations of Radioengineering
Novosibirsk State Technical University, NSTU
Novosibirsk, Russia

Abstract—**This article discusses a dual-channel system with motion sensors based on inverse filtering and a dual-channel system based on the Wiener filter.**

Keywords—Multichannel structures, sensors, inverse filtration, Wiener filter, noise

I.   INTRODUCTION

Multichannel structures using additional sensors are often used to attenuate the noise in the informational-measuring systems. The operation of the sensors is based on the principles of the various physical nature. One of the channels, hereinafter called the main channel, generates the useful effect. The other channels, called additional channels, are used to mitigate the noise in the main channel. A significant effect are able to achieve even when using only one additional channel. Multichannel structures are used in cases where the required quality of a signal can not be achieved by using noise filtering in the main channel [1].

II.   THE PROBLEM STATEMENT

Measurement sensors in the main and the additional channels are based on different physical principles and this leads to the fact that the useful effect which is presented in the main channel, is absent in the additional channel, and some types of noises in the main and the additional channel are correlated. Therefore, the use of additional sensors helps to estimate the noise in the additional channel without useful effect, which is presented in the main channel and modify the signal of the additional channel to the form of the useful signal in the main channel. The subtraction of these two signals helps to attenuate the noise in the main channel.

The informational white Gaussian noise ξ_i is common source of the noise for both channels from which the measuring systems form the observed noise in the channels x_i and y_i. All processes occur in discrete time $-\infty < i < \infty$. There are white Gaussian noise in recording devices δ_i and η_i and the useful signal s_i in the main channel, which estimation is the ultimate objective of measurement system.

Adaptive converter is based on analysis of signals $\hat{y}_i = y_i + \eta_i$ and $\hat{x}_i = x_i + \delta_i + s_i$ and converts the first one so that

x_i^* signal characteristics at its output matches with similar characteristics of x_i. In this case, the output error $\varepsilon_i = \hat{x}_i - x_i^*$ mitigate the noise in x_i.

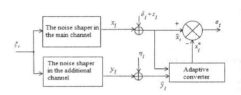

Fig. 1.   The formation and noise compensation in two-channel measurement system

The noises x_i and y_i are often described as a Gaussian models in real measurement systems and, therefore, the shapers, presented in Fig. 1, are linear transducers. The conversion can be represented as:

$$x_i = L_x(\Xi), \; y_i = L_y(\Xi),$$

Ξ - vector of input samples of white noise. Suppose that the following expression describes the inverse transformation for the additional channel:

$$\xi_i = L_y^{-1}(\mathbf{Y}) \qquad (1)$$

where $\mathbf{Y}$ - the vector consisting of samples y_i. We will find the estimation $\hat{\xi}_i$ of the white noise ξ_i, applying the transformation (1) the observed signal $\hat{y}_i$:

$$\hat{\xi}_i = L_y^{-1}(\hat{\mathbf{Y}}) \qquad (2)$$

where $\hat{\mathbf{Y}}$ - the vector consisting of samples of the observed signal $\hat{y}_i$. Carrying out further transformation, we will find the noise estimation in the main channel:

$$x_i^* = L_x(\hat{\Xi}) \qquad (2+)$$

where $\hat{\Xi}$ - the vector of estimates of the white noise $\hat{\xi}_i$, which is received by the inverse transformation of the additional channel. The estimation x_i^* does not match the exact value of x_i because of the noise influence η_i in the additional channel.

Inverse transformer of the additional channel was used because of simplicity its of implementation. Inverse filtering does not give very good results in the presence of noise, because this method does not take into account the noise effects. Wiener filtering methods, which take into account a priori knowledge of the statistical properties of the noise field, can improve the quality of the corrected signals. Therefore we consider the transformer of the additional channel based on Wiener filtering.

The transfer function of the Wiener filter has the form:

$$\tilde{H}_{wien}(\omega) = \frac{\tilde{H}^*(\omega)}{\left|\tilde{H}(\omega)\right|^2 + \dfrac{\hat{G}_\eta(\omega)}{\hat{G}_y(\omega)}}$$

where $\hat{G}_\eta(\omega)$, $\hat{G}_y(\omega)$ - power spectral densities periodically continued of the noise and the original signal, ()* - the symbol of complex conjugation, $H(\omega)$ - the frequency response of distorting system.

The frequency response of distorting system is:

$$\tilde{H}(\omega) = H_{inv.ad}(\omega) \cdot H_{main}(\omega) = \frac{H_{main}(\omega)}{H_{ad}(\omega)}$$

The system function of the filter that forms the process of the white noise is:

$$H_{main}(z) = \frac{1}{1 + \sum\limits_{j=1}^{J} A_j \cdot z^{-j}}$$

$$H_{ad}(z) = \frac{1}{1 + \sum\limits_{k=1}^{K} B_k \cdot z^{-k}}$$

where A and B - Yule-Walker linear prediction coefficients for the main and the additional channels, respectively, z^{-j}, z^{-k} - z - transformation.

$$H_{main}(z) = \frac{1}{1 + \sum\limits_{j=1}^{J} A_j \cdot e^{-j2\pi\frac{ij}{N}}}$$

$$H_{ad}(z) = \frac{1}{1 + \sum\limits_{k=1}^{K} B_k \cdot e^{-j2\pi\frac{ik}{N}}}$$

where N - the signal length (in samples), j, k - number of the prediction order.

III. RESULTS

The analysis of the efficiency of the described complexation methods is performed using simulation. It was based on records of two coordinate electronic gyroscope signals, which examples are shown in Fig. 2 and Fig. 3. One of the signals (Fig. 2) was considered as a prototype of signal of the main channel of the measuring system, the second (Fig. 3) – as the additional channel signal.

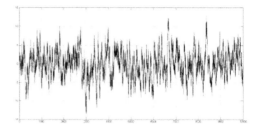

Fig. 2. The prototype of the main channel signal

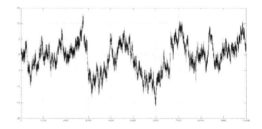

Fig. 3. The prototype of the additional channel signal

The estimates of the prediction parameters $\mathbf{A} = \left\|a_1, a_2, ..., a_J\right\|^T$, $\mathbf{B} = \left\|b_1, b_2, ..., b_K\right\|^T$ were based on the real signals using the Yule-Walker 8-order prediction method and were used for signals simulation and processing.

Fig. 4 shows signals fragments obtained in the experiment at the relative noise level $\overline{\eta^2/y^2} = 0,5$ in the additional channel. The continuous curve corresponds to the signal of the main channel, the dashed curve corresponds to additional channel and the dash-dot line shows the signal after bringing the signal of the additional channel to the form of the main channel using the Wiener filter. The high conversion efficiency can be qualitatively seen.

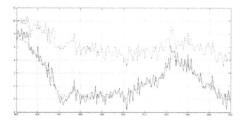

Fig. 4. Fragments of signals of the main channel and the additional channel before and after bringing it to the form of the main channel

The main results of the simulation are shown in Fig. 5 in the form of dependence of the relative compensation error $\overline{\varepsilon_i^2}/\overline{x_i^2} = \overline{(x_i - x_i^*)^2}/\overline{x_i^2}$ from the relative level of noise $\overline{\eta^2}/\overline{y^2}$ in the additional channel, where the dash above denotes the expectation operation. Curve 1 corresponds to the inverse filter; curve 2 corresponds to the Wiener filter.

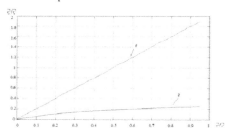

Fig. 5. Dependence of the mean square error compensation on the level of the noise in the additional channel

IV. CONCLUSION

The level of the output error increases proportionally to noise level in the additional channel and makes it difficult use this method even at relatively low noise levels. The error compensation is significantly lower, while using non-cau Wiener filter, whereupon its use in practical systems see promising.

REFERENCES

[1] Widrow B., Stearns P.N. Adaptive Signal Processing, Prentice H 1985 (Transl. Russ., Moscow: Radio i svjaz, Publ. 1989, 440 p.)

[2] Gruzman I.S., Kirichuk V.S., Kosyh V.P., Peretjagin G.I., Spektor A Digital image processing in information systems: textbook, Novosibi NSTU, 2002, 352 p.

[3] Pratt W.K. Digital Image Processing, New York: John Wiley & Sc 1978. (Transl. Russ., Moscow: Mir, Publ. 1982. 2nd book, 480 p.)

[4] Marple, S. L. Digital Spectral Analysis. Englewood Cliffs, NJ: Prem Hall, 1987. (Transl. Russ., Moscow, Mir, Publ. 1990, 584 p.)

HARDWARE ACCELERATED SENSING FOR FAULT DETECTION AND SAFETY

ASSESSMENT OF TURBO GENERATORS

Yanjin Altankhuyag,
Technische Universität Chemnitz
Computer Engineering Professorship
Prof. Dr. Wolfram Hardt,
Professorship Computer Engineering Department of Technische Universität Chemnitz

Abstract

With the rapid development of sensor technology, various professional sensors are installed on modern machinery to monitor operational processes and assure operational safety, which play an important role in industry. On the basis of a professional sensor and the corresponding system, sensor-dependent vibration signals are acquired and analyzed by a second generation wavelet package, which reflects time-varying operational characteristic of individual machinery. Derived from the sensor-dependent signals' wavelet energy distribution over the observed signal frequency range, wavelet Rényi entropy is defined to compute the operational uncertainty of a turbo generator, which is then associated with its operational safety degree.
Keywords: operational safety assessment, turbo generator, sensor-dependent, vibration signal, second generation wavelet package, vibration analysis, failure detection, FPGA

1. Instruction

Turbo generators are a key part of power systems which have found increasing service in the power industry throughout the world. They can produce a great amount of electrical energy depending on their size and weight. They usually require regular upkeep and scheduled maintenance. With aging generator units and mechanical components, safety assessment is one of the most important and imperative indicators for a plant to prevent failures. Safety refers to the ability of a system or component to perform its required function under stated conditions for a specified period of time without accidents, which is very important for industrial enterprises to protect
running reliability against damage, faults, failures and economic losses. Therefore, safety is studied worldwide by many researchers and
engineers. Matteson proposed a dynamic multi-criteria optimization framework for
sustainability and reliability assessments of power systems [2]. Since turbo generator faults have a significant impact on safety, Whyatt *et al.* identified failure modes experienced by turbo generators and described their reliability [5]. Tsvetkov *et al.* presented a mathematical model for

analysis of generator reliability, including development of defects [6]. Monitoring the condition of a component is typically based on several sensors that estimate the values of some measurable parameters (signals) and triggering a fault alarm when the measured signal is out of limit. Many techniques have been developed for fault detection early. Besides detecting fault and safety assessment there is the necessity of low cost instrumentation for measurement and analysis. In recent years, intensive research effort has been focused on the technique of fault diagnosis and can be summarized:

- Time and frequency domain analysis
- Time domain analysis of the electromagnetic torque and flux phasor
- Temperature measurement, infrared recognition, radio frequency (RF) emission monitoring
- Motor current signature analysis (MCSA)
- Detection by space vector angular fluctuation (SVAF)
- Noise and vibration monitoring
- Acoustic noise measurement
- Harmonic analysis of motor torque and speed
- Model, artificial intelligence and neural network based techniques.

Vibrations are natural processes in electrical rotary machines and are created by same dynamic forces. Here we will focus vibration analysis and operational safety evaluation based on wavelet entropy form sensor dependent vibration signal. Firstly, the sensor-dependent vibration signals reflecting the time varying characteristic of an individual turbo generator are acquired by sensors and the analyzed by the second generation wavelet package since the wavelet transform excels in analyzing unsteady signals in both the time domain and frequency domain. Derived from the sensor dependent signal wavelet energy distribution over the observed frequency range, wavelet entropy will define to compute the operational uncertainty.

II. Theoretical Background

First we will look the techniques that have been developed to detect fault, where the MVSA and vibration analysis. Next, a brief for operation assessment of wavelet entropy from sensor dependent vibration signal.

The MCSA technique is based on the stator current at the motor to further correlate the measured signal with the specific fault analysis. Here are two variations for this signal analysis: 1. Based in steady state analysis and 2) based on startup transient analysis. Steady state analysis is used to detect broken rotor bars, air gap eccentricity, bearing damage, load effect using sideband frequencies that appear in the current spectrum when the motor is damaged. Another way of MCSA analysis is represented, where they detect failures such as open phase or short circuits by using the discrete wavelet transform.

MCSA technique provides good result on fault detection; yet every fault needs an especially devoted instrumentation system and algorithm for failure detection. On the other hand, vibration analysis can be used as general technique for fault detection because almost all of motor failures are reflected as vibration changes. Vibration signal analysis is employed to detect different kinds of faults by using FFT as the mathematical tool MATLAB. Also, where both the vibration spectrum and current spectrum are computed and the detect fault. Paper has the possibility of detecting different kinds of faults in motor by obtaining the vibration spectrum n steady state, and then a operation safety assessment with wavelet entropy from sensor dependent vibration signal.

II.1 Faults and Vibration relationship

There are many kinds of failures that can be detected using vibration analysis: these kinds of faults have been classified according to their origin as electrical or mechanical and according to their location as rotor or stator. In addition, well known research has established the relationship between machine faults and some harmonic components.

Table1 Possible faults related vibration frequency

Frequency	Possible Failure
1xRPM	Unbalance, looseness, misalignment of gear or pulley, resonance, electrical problems, alternative forces
2xRPM	Mechanical offset, misalignment, alternative forces, resonance
3xRPM	Misalignment, axial mechanical breath
<1xRPM	Slip, oil whirl
Supply frequency	Electrical problems
RPM	Broken bars, damaged gears, aerodynamic forces, hydraulic

	forces, mechanical set alternative forces

Table1 shows the association between common faults and its corresponding vibration frequencies. Spectrum postprocessing consist of analyzing the region of the spectrum where the fault is expected, as stated table1, to give a single value as weighting parameter. Basically, the a certain bandlimited region of the vibration spectrum as input from one of the vibration sensor dependent channel. As well as the selected mathematical technique to analyze the region of the spectrum where the fault is located, for the particular case of unbalance detection as shown in Table1. At the same time, the amplitude thresholds are adjusted to automatically determine, based on mathematical form of a weighted accumulation. The algorithm to obtain a weighting parameter can be used and implemented into the FPGA, due to its configurability. Selected algorithm to obtain the weighting parameter by accumulation of region on the spectrum is accurately sufficient to detect the analyzed faults. Thus

$$A = \sum_{k=LI}^{LS} a_j P_{xx}^B(k)$$

P_{xx}^B	vibration signal spectrum
a_j	spectrum gain;
j	gain index;
A	accumulation result;
k	frequency index;
LI	lower limit from the selected range
LS	upper limit from the selected range

III. FPGA implementation

The system will be two main block, namely the instrumentation system and the embedded system into an FPGA. The instrumentation system consists of accelerometer (three axis) implemented into a micro electro mechanical sensors and the data acquisition (DAQ). The FPGA embedded system contains different blocks: DAQ drivers in charge of controlling the communication between the acquisition system and FPGA. A video graphics array (VGA) unit is included for spectrum visualization without needing a PC; additionally an RS232 block will include for optional communication with a PC of required by the application for operational assessment.

IV Second generation wavelet package transform

Since the second generation wavelet package transform obeys the energy conservation principle due to its bi-orthogonal basis, each of the attained $2l$ frequency bands has the same bandwidth and end to end after the lth decomposition and reconstruction. Supposing $sl,i(k)$ is the reconstructed signal at the lth decomposition in the

lth frequency band, its energy E_l,i and relative energy $\tilde{E}^-l,i$ are respectively defined as follows:

$$E_{l,i} = \frac{1}{n-1}\sum_{k=1}^{n}(s_{l,i}(k))^2 \qquad i = 1,2\ldots,2^l, \quad k = 1,2,\ldots,n, n \in Z \qquad (1)$$

$$\tilde{E}_{l,i} = E_{l,i}\left(\sum_{i=1}^{2^l} E_{l,i}\right)^{-1} \qquad (2)$$

where, $\sum_{i=1}^{2^l} \tilde{E}_{l,i} = 1$, the sum of total relative energy equals to one.

IV Operational Safety degree with wavelet entropy Renyi from sensor dependent vibration signals

The operational safety degree with wavelet Rényi entropy R from sensor-dependent vibration signals is defined as:

$$R = 1 - \frac{1}{1-\alpha}log_{2^l}\sum_{i=1}^{2^l}\tilde{E}^{\alpha} \qquad (3)$$

where the parameter $\alpha \in [0,1) \cup (1,\infty)$.

An illustration of the proposed operational safety assessment method with wavelet Rényi entropy is presented in figure 1, which mainly includes condition monitoring and signal acquisition, signal processing with second generation wavelet package transform and operational safety assessment with wavelet Rényi entropy.

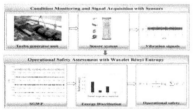

Figure 1: Illustration of safety assessment from sensor dependent vibration signal

V. Fault diagnosis

As the above analysis, the amplitude of the running frequency is the largest among the whole frequency range and some harmonic frequency components from two times the running frequency to ten times the running frequency are also large.

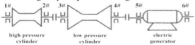

high pressure cylinder   low pressure cylinder   electric generator

Figure 2: The structure diagram of the turbo generator unit (50MW)

Signals analyzed by the second generation wavelet package and wavelet package energy distributions

in level 2, level 3 and level 4 exhibit non-stationary, nonlinear and colored noise characteristics.

Considering the start-up process with no load and loading operation conditions, the vertical vibrations of the #3 and #5 bearings which are adjacent to the #4 bearing are not high (under 20 m). Different from the #3 and #5 bearings, the vibration of the #4 bearing increases with increased speed and load. It is concluded that the vibration is not caused by imbalance and misalignment for the reason that vibrations would be out of limits in multiple bearing position if an imbalance or misalignment fault occurs. Therefore, the problem is focused on the #4 bearing itself. It is inferred that the monitored non-stationary and nonlinear components in the vibration signal of the #4 bearing may be caused by mechanical looseness and local friction, so the bearing force and support status of the sizing block and bearing lodgement must be checked.

With the above analysis, the turbo generator unit is stopped and overhauled. The preload of the #4 bearing bushing is about 0.11 mm, which is far from the requirement of 0.25 mm. The gaps of the left and right sizing block are checked by a filler gauge. The 0.05 mm filler gauge can be filled into 30 mm of the left sizing block and 25 mm of the right sizing block. The gap in the bottom of the #4 bearing bushing is also far away from the obligate gap of 0.05 mm. Therefore, the gaps of the 4# bearing bush are re-corrected and the preload is added to the requirement of 0.25 mm.

After maintenance, the turbo generator unit is operated again. The sensor-dependent vibration signal is decreased in the start-up process with increasing speed. The peak to peak vibration in the vertical direction in the #4 bearing bushing is about 40~55 μm with a load of 45 MW, which is much better than before. In order to assess the operational safety of the turbo generator unit after maintenance, vibration monitoring via sensors is conducted in a stable speed of 3000 r/min with a load of 6 MW, which is as the same as the case before maintenance. The waveform of the acquired vibration signal shown in Figure 4 shows some differences compared with the vibration signal before maintenance in Figure 3 such as the symmetry between the top and bottom of the vibration signal is much better than before and the peak to peak vibration is about 45 μm, which falls in the permissible range. The amplitudes of the harmonic frequency components from two times the running frequency to ten times the running frequency are decreased. The second generation wavelet package is adopted to analyze the acquired vibration signal on level 2, level 3 and level 4, respectively. Afterwards, the relative energy of the corresponding frequency band analyzed by the second generation wavelet package is computed according to the Equation (2).

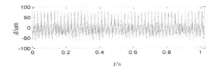

Figure 2: the waveform of the sensor dependent vibration signal in the time domain.

Figure 3: the waveform of the sensor dependent vibration signal in time domain after maintenance

Conclusions

The work consist of developing a low cost vibration analyzer able to carry out online multichannel monitoring and provide and automatic diagnosis. Also, a method of safety assessment based on wavelet entropy from sensor dependent vibration signal is proposed for turbo generators. The vibration signals are analyzed by mean of second generation wavelet package. Deriving from the signal's wavelet energy distribution over the observed frequency range, the wavelet Renyi entropy is defined to compute the operational uncertainty, which is the transformed into an safety degree. The safety as influenced by the decomposition level 1 of the second generation wavelet package possible to analyze and set at an appropriate level. Since timely maintenance can increase the operational safety and avoid the occurrence of accidents, the proposed faults can be detected. Contribution is FGA for developing a multichannel vibration analyzer with postprocessing stage which allows providing an automatic diagnosis on in the state of the continuous online monitoring.

References
[1]P.Bilski and W. Winiecki, "Virtual spectrum analyzer based on data acquisition card," IEEE trans. Instrum.Meas., vol.51, no 1,pp82-87
[2] Matteson S. Methods for multi-criteria sustainability and reliability assessments of power systems. Energy. 2014;71:130–136.
[3]. Lo Prete C., Hobbs B.F., Norman C.S., Cano-Andrade S., Fuentes A., von Spakovsky M.R., Mili L. Sustainability and reliability assessment of microgrids in a regional electricity market. Energy. 2012;41:192–202.

[4]. Moharil R.M., Kulkani P.S. Generator system reliability analysis including wind generators using hourly mean wind speed. Electr. Power Compon. Syst. 2008;36:1–16.
[5]. Whyatt P., Horrocks P., Mills L. Steam generator reliability—Implications for apwr codes end standards. Nucl. Energy. 1995;34:217–228.
[6]. Tsvetkov V.A. A mathematical-model for analysis of generator reliability, including development of defects. Electr. Technol. 1992:107–112.
[7]. Sun Y., Wang P., Cheng L., Liu H. Operational reliability assessment of power systems considering condition-dependent failure rate. IET Gener. Transm. Dis. 2010;4:60–72.
[8]. Baraldi P., Di Maio F., Pappaglione L., Zio E., Seraoui R. Condition monitoring of electrical power plant components during operational transients. Proc. Inst. Mech. Eng. Part O J. Risk Reliab. 2012;226:568–583.
[9]. Dumoulin C., Karaiskos G., Sener J.Y., Deraemaeker A. Online monitoring of cracking in concrete structures using embedded piezoelectric transducers. Smart Mater. Struct. 2014;23 doi: 10.1088/0964-1726/23/11/115016. [Cross Ref]
[10]. Qiu L., Yuan S.F., Chang F.K., Bao Q., Mei H.F. On-line updating gaussian mixture model for aircraft wing spar damage evaluation under time-varying boundary condition. Smart Mater. Struct. 2014;23 doi: 10.1088/0964-1726/23/12/125001. [Cross Ref]
[11]. Lu F., Huang J.Q., Xing Y.D. Fault diagnostics for turbo-shaft engine sensors based on a simplified on-board model. Sensors. 2012;12:11061–11076. [PMC free article] [PubMed]
[12]. Li Z.J., Liu Y., Liu F.X., Yang X.J. Hybrid reliability model of hydraulic turbine-generator unit based on nonlinear vibration. Proc. Inst. Mech. Eng. Part C J. Mech. Eng. Sci. 2014;228:1880–1887.
[13]. Hua C., Zhang Q., Xu G.H., Zhang Y.Z., Xu T. Performance reliability estimation method based on adaptive failure threshold. Mech. Syst. Signal Process. 2013;36:505–519.
[14]. Canovas J.S., Kupka J. On the topological entropy on the space of fuzzy numbers. Fuzzy Set Syst. 2014;257:132–145.
[15]. Celik T. Spatial entropy-based global and local image contrast enhancement. IEEE Trans. Image Process. 2014;23:5298–5308. [PubMed]

Development of Wireless PGN Analyzer for ISOBUS Network

Enkhbaatar Tumenjargal[†], Luubaatar Badarch[†*], Woonchul Ham[*], Enkhzul Doopalam[†], Amartuvshin Togooch[†],

[†] School of Information and Communications Technology, Mongolian University of Science and Technology, Ulaanbaatar, Mongolia
[*] Chonbuk National University, Chollabuk-do, Jeonju, South Korea
[†] enkhbaatar79@gmail.com, [†*] luubaatar@gmail.com, [*] wcham@jbnu.ac.kr

Abstract— Communication between ECUs (Electronic Control Units) in agricultural machineries tends to use ISO11783 widely, that is PGN (Parameter Group Number) based communication protocol lays on CAN protocol by altering its identifier part. Messages in line are transferred and received between ECUs according to ISO11783 standard. This paper discusses about design of wireless monitoring system. We used an ARM Cortex-M3 microcontroller embedded development board and marvel8686 wireless module. The wireless ISOBUS monitoring system, attached to communication line, reads messages, interpret them, and display them on the screen in easily comprehendible form. It can be used to generate messages and monitor the traffic on physical bus systems. The monitoring system connected to ECUs, monitor and simulate real traffic of communication and functionality of the ECUs. In order to support our work, we have implemented the monitoring tool. The development consists of two parts: GUI of the application and firmware level programming. Hence the monitoring system is attached to the communication line and equipped by Wi-Fi module; farmer/dispatcher in a farm monitors all messages in communication line on personal computer and smart device.

Keywords— ISO 11783, PGN, CAN, Wi-Fi, ARM Cortex-M3.

I. Introduction

Agricultural machinery control is an interdisciplinary field of study concerning the integration of mechanics, electronics, and software engineering expertise. Today a new generation of tractors exists with capabilities so advanced they can be assumed in many of the roles and responsibilities once entrusted to their human counterparts. This evolution in tractors is the direct result of continuing research advancements among its constituent disciplines. The ISO 11783 [11]~[16][17] standard has and, continues to be, an active area of research within the agricultural engineering community.

The ISO 11783 standard was jointly developed by tractor and implements manufacturers including the AGCO Corporation [18], AGROCOM [19], DICKEY-Jonh Corporation [20], Deere & Company [21], and Müller-Elektronik [22]. These manufacturers have also created a specification defining how this standard should be recognized. This specification is commonly known as ISOBUS. All packets, except for the request PGN and address claim packets, contain eight bytes of data and standard header which contains an index called parameter group number (PGN), which is embedded in the CAN

message's 29-bit identifier [1-3]. A PGN identifies a message's function and associated data [4-6]. To implement and develop the networked tractor system we need to analyze and control all messages in communication line.

This paper is organized as follows: In section 2, 3, 4 and 5, we have described an overview of standards, test environment, embedded workbench applications, workbench results and discussion, respectively. Finally, conclusions are presented in section 6.

II. An overview of standards

The ISO 11783 is a new standard for electronic communications protocol for tractors and machinery in agriculture and forestry. This ISO 11783 standard is sometimes called as ISOBUS [1]-[2]. The network has messages defined to allow communications between any of the components, like communication between the Virtual Terminal, the Task Controller, the GPS ECU and other ECUs.

It consists of several parts: general standard for mobile data communication, physical layer, data link layer, network layer, network management, virtual terminal, implement messages applications layer, power train messages, tractor ECU, task controller and management information system for data interchange, mobile data element dictionary, diagnostic and file server. The structure of electronic data communication according to ISO 11783 is based on the open system interconnect (OSI) model layers, however, the higher functional layers sometimes defined differently.

The purpose of ISO 11783 is to provide an open, interconnected system for on-board electronic systems. It is intended to enable electronic control units (ECUs) to communicate with each other, providing a standardized system. The tractor ECU shall have at least one node for connection to the implement bus.

For this purpose we implemented ISOBUS PGN analyzer in the previous work. When a PGN analyzer reads data from the ISOBUS it needs to know how to interpret what it is seeing and display the output in an easy to read format. It can be used to generate and monitor the traffic on physical bus systems. In order to support our work, we have implemented the PGN analyzer tool for personal computer. To advance our PGN analyzer we developed web based application in STM32F103 development board with wireless module for smart devices. The general architecture of our development system is shown in figure 1.

31

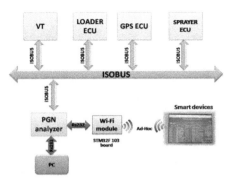

Figure 1. General architecture of development system

Development of analyzer consists of three parts: GUI of application in personal computer, web based application in development board and firmware level programming.

III. Hardware design of ISOBUS PGN analyzer

The PGN analyzer is implemented on the embedded board it's main CPU is 32 bit, 72MHz CortexM3 cored STM32F107 development board with two CAN interfaces. Once development board of analyzer has two serial interfaces we use one serial interface for the communication between the analyzer and application program in PC and communication between analyzer and wi-fi development board for smart devices. The CAN1 channel is used to monitor the ISOBUS. However, CAN2 channel can be used as well, if there is need of monitoring two ISOBUSs. The status information of the PGN analyzer is depicted on the LCD display of the board. We can see the appearance of the PGN analyzer in the Fig. 2. Here ISOBUS connected PGN analyzer and sample ECUs are depicted. We implemented sample ECUs, for example: GPS sensor, lighting, sprayer, tractor ECU and VT.

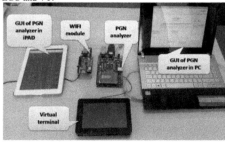

Figure 2. PGN analyzer connected with ISOBUS ECUs

IV. Firmware level programming

For the application program of GPS sensor, we used an open source programming library named ISOAgLib. The

IsoAgLib is a C++ library in development of ISO 11783 standard applications in an Object Oriented way to serve as a software layer between application specific program and communication protocol details. The author of IsoAgLib library, Dipl. - Inform. Achim Spangler, licensed with exceptions under the terms of the GNU General Public License (GPL). The simple function calls for jobs like starting a measuring program for a process data value on a remote ECU, the main program has not to deal with single CAN message formatting. This way communication problem between ECU's which use this library should be prevented. The IsoAgLib has a modular design pursuant to the various functional components of the standard ISO 11783. The library has this design to make sure the minimum use of IsoAgLib in program memory of Implement ECU. The IsoAgLib demonstrates the layered architecture to be easily familiar with new hardware platforms. Most of the software can be used without alteration on all platforms. The layered architecture is described by the diagram in Figure 3.

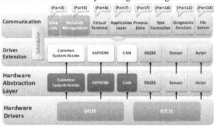

Figure 3. System architecture of embedded workbench applications

The IsoAgLib was developed to be suitable with different systems, and these systems can be an element of processor, memory, Human Machine Interface (HMI) and interface with the CAN bus. Therefore, the IsoAgLib is divided into two sections: the library itself and HAL. The HAL is responsible for communicating with the operating system (OS) or BIOS device that is running the application, as can be seen in Fig.3. We implement CAN-bus in real-time operating system. Here the application program initialized CAN controller and accessing CAN-bus.

The hardware programming is implemented in the firmware level. The Fig. 4 shows the main structure of firmware level program. PGN analyzer's firmware program has been five main functions:

- Receive data from the personal computer via RS232 and the ISOBUS via CAN[1] interface

- Processing received data both RS232 and CAN interface

- Processed data send to the personal computer via RS232 and the ISOBUS via CAN interface

- Processed data send to the wi-fi development board via RS232 interface

- Wifi development board display processed data in

web based application for smart devices

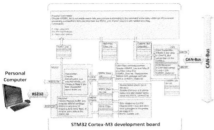

Figure 4. Main algorithm of the buffering method between RS232 and CAN-bus

Receiver side recognizes and accumulates RS232 data into one CAN packet. Application program and firmware program has the predefined structure of data sequence to send and receive CAN package, control and status data.

Receiving part of the firmware program's RS232 data sequence recognition and accumulation process is shown in the Fig.5.

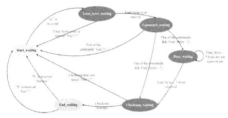

Figure 5. State machine diagram of PGN analyzer

There are six steps, we can see from the Fig.4; start waiting, total bytes waiting, command waiting, data waiting, checksum waiting and end waiting.

During RS232 data sequence receiving function, the Cortex-M3 CPU monitors via SYSTICK time counting value, in order to recognize data loss from the PC. The waiting time is 200 ms, which is allowed to wait for the next expectable byte. If there no byte is received anymore in 200ms, receiving status shifts in to *start_waiting* state and losses all the in complete bytes that are received yet. The CAN receiver receives and checks the CAN packet from the CAN1 peripheral of the STM32F107 which is allowed to be sent to the PC by filtering with the PGN values in the filter list.

If the packet is allowed, it is repackaged into RS232 data sequence to be sent to the PC: adding head and tail of the sequence ('@'and '$'), command ('T'), number of total bytes and checksum.

Another function of the firmware is to inform the status of the hardware to the application program via RS232 per second. It sends the status with command 'L' (device is alive-status) per second. Therefore, application program

can easily recognize whether the hardware is functioning or not at moment.

V. Graphical User Interface of PGN Analyzer

There are two graphic user interfaces. One is dedicated for the personal computer which is implemented in the Borland Delphi 7.0[10] environment with the object oriented Pascal language. Another GUI is for smart or mobile device is developed in HTML5. Delphi is effective to develop this kind of system, because it has rapid application development (RAD) interface and good tool to help against the developing mistakes which cause understanding problems.

The GUI of PGN analyzer program's backbone some application programs running for parsing RS232 serial data to convert CAN packet and reverse procedure. We used the CAN server, CAN messenger, and CAN logalizer console application tools for parsing CAN packets, those original made from the IsoAglib. In this parsing procedure using named pipes to connect a GUI to a console application in windows environment.

Named pipes allow two processes to share data bi-directionally synchronously or asynchronously. This makes them ideal for putting a GUI front-end on a console application. Software developers usually provide a rich GUI to easily run an application in a desktop environment. However, users sometimes prefer a console application that typically provides access to the fullest range of application options via console interface and may be composed into a pipeline of user interface-less processing steps. The Fig. 6 illustrates received CAN packet parsing procedure until GUI. We capture serial data from RS232 interface then convert to CAN messenger in understandable format.

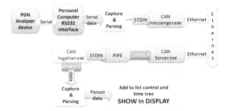

Figure 6. Received CAN packet parsing procedure shown in GUI

The CAN messenger sends to the CAN server by using Ethernet network. The CAN server console application program's standard output connected the virtual pipe. The pipe connected to CAN logalizer [8] console application's standard input. The logalizer analysis standard input data and interpreting user understandable format. Finaly, those interpreted data parsed then add to list control and tree control.

Figure 7. Transmitted CAN packet shown in GUI

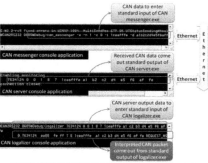

Figure 8. CAN packet parsing and interpreting procedure in the command line

Transmitting procedure is similarly the receiving in GUI. The Fig.7 and 8 are shown in the block diagram of transmission procedure for PGN analyzer. The sample received CAN packets interprets is shown in the Fig.9.

Figure 9. Sample captured data from our PGN analyzer device

The GUI software of personal computer is written in object oriented Pascal only runs under the Windows operational system, shown in Fig.10.

Figure 10. GUI of the PGN Analyzer

VI. Transplant of Embedded Web Server

The several embedded web servers are being intensively studied in the world, we develop GoAhead web server for GUI of smart or mobile devices. The reasons of our choice of GoAhead are followings:

- Small memory footprint
- Configurable security model
- Supporting the generation of dynamic Web page content
- Support for devices that do not have a file system
- Portability across a wide range of platforms and CPU architectures
- Integration of the source code into very customized devices

Figure.11 is shows the system diagram of embedded web server and STM32F10x ARM Cortex-M3 development board.

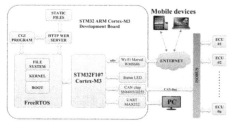

Figure 11. The system diagram of embedded web server

First of all, briefly mention about general procedure of transplantation of embedded software. It consists of three main parts: first one is bootLoader which is the code that firstly run when power on, second one is kernel code which determines process scheduling, inter-process communication, memory management, network and file interface, last one is file system that manages the logical file, including the provision of file operation. Either case code has to be written in pc then generated binary code using the cross-compiler [23]. After that binary code has to be downloaded to the embedded board. To add new application to the embedded system we have to transplant executable file to the file system image of embedded system. Embedded web server for the embedded devices provide network interface, to realize the remote management and control, which is an important technology of networked embedded system [1]. As mentioned before, to control any device by embedded web server we used common gateway interface (CGI) application program [25]-[27]. The main role of CGI application is to transmit the corresponding implementation result to the client browser after completing the relevant operations and the operations to the bottom hardware to let the users see the results of the implementation of operation intuitively.

To transplant web server to the embedded device we follow next steps:
- Download web server source code from web site
- Decompress the downloaded source code
- Create make file
- Check and fix cross-compiler version and path
- Create executable file of Web server
- Create *cgi.c* code for the your usage
- Compile and create executable file of cgi_app
- Copy created executable files to /system/bin/ director of kernel
- Create html web page for controlling
- Copy created html files to /system/www/ director of kernel
- Recompile or create system image
- Download system image to embedded board
- Reboot embedded board
- Configure ip address and load web server in browser and run it.

The web based GUI of wireless analyzer is written in HTML5. The main interfaces for the user are shown in the Fig 12.

Figure 12. Web based GUI of the PGN Analyzer

VII. Conclusions and Future Works

In this paper we present the hardware and software development of wireless ISO11783 parameter group number (PGN) analyzer device that is implemented in

STM32F107VC Cortex-M3 development board with the Wi-Fi module. In programming of ISO11783 PGN analyzer, we focused on both of firmware and GUI on the monitoring computer and smart devices. The main role of the firmware programming is capturing CAN packet and converting to RS232 serial data format or receiving RS232 data from computer, convert it into CAN data and send. GUI of PGN analyzer receives RS232 data and converting to CAN packets in order to monitor. Those converted CAN packets are sent to some of hidden application programs using pipe programming technique. We used two virtual pipes for parsing and interpreting CAN packets. Finally parsed and interpreted data is shown on GUI of PGN analyzer in ISO11783 standard form. All converting, parsing and interpreting procedures are simultaneously made in two development boards, final displaying GUIs are different. GUIs are written in Delphi programming language and HTML5. Hence our web based application is written in HTML5 which has a good opportunity to support other mobile devices. Recently advances in wireless sensor networking (WSN) technology have led to the development of low cost, low power consumptions, multifunctional sensor nodes. With these advances, near future our research focused on wireless networks in ISOBUS has emerged. Fig.14 is shown development environments of our system.

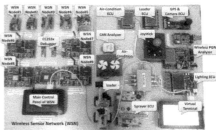

Figure 14. A Development of Environment for ISOBUS and Wireless Sensor Networks

REFERENCES

[1] Robert Bosch, GmbH, "CAN specification," *Germany*, 1991.
[2] E. Tumenjargal, L. Badarch, H. Kwon, and W. Ham, "Embedded software and hardware implementation system for a human machine interface based on ISOAgLib," *Journal of Zhejiang University-Science C-Computers & Electronics*, vol. 14, pp. 155-166, Mar 2013.
[3] K. Hyeokjae, T. Enkhbaatar, and H. Woonchul, "Implementation of Virtual Terminal Based on CAN by Using WinCE Platform Builder 6.0," *Key Engineering Materials*, vol. 480, pp. 938-943, 2011.
[4] W. Ham, T. Enkhbaatar, B. Luubaatar and K. Hyeokjae, "Implementation of ECU for Agricultural Machines Based on ISOAgLib Open Source", presented at the 11th Int. Conf. Precision Agriculture, Indianapolis, Indiana, USA, Jul. 15-18, 2012.
[5] T.Enkhbaatar, B.Luubaatar, K.Hyeokjae and W.Ham, "Design and Implementation of Virtual Terminal Based on ISO11783 Standard for Agricultural Tractors," presented at the 11th Int. Conf. Precision Agriculture, Indianapolis, Indiana, USA, Jul. 15-18, 2012.

[6]   E. Tumenjargal, L. Badarch, K. Hyeokjae, and W. Ham, "Software Development Tool for Agricultural Machinery Based on IsoAgLib Open Source Library," presented at the 2012 ASABE Annual Meeting, Dallas, Texas, USA, Jul. 29 – August 1, 2012.

[7]   Md. M. K. Sarker, D. Park, W. Ham, E. Tumenjargal, and J. Lee, "Embedded Workbench Applications of GPS Sensor for Agricultural Tractor," presented at the WorldComp'12, Las Vegas, Nevada, USA, Jul. 16-19, 2012.

[8]   A. Spangler and M. Wodok, "IsoAgLib–Development of ISO 11783 Applications in an Object Oriented way," ed, 2010.

[9]   S. Ingle, S. Dessai, and R. Gore, "Development of Software for CANlog Device to Determine the Performance of Tractor", International Journal of Recent Trends in Engineering, Vol. 1, No. 3, May, 2009.

[10] G. Craessaerts, K. Maertens, and J. De Baerdemaeker, "A Windows-based design environment for combine automation via CANbus", Journal of Computers and Electronics in Agriculture, pp. 233–245, 2005.

[11] ISO 11783-1, "Tractors and machinery for agriculture and forestry - Serial control and communications data network," Part 1: General standard for mobile data communication, International Organization for Standardization, 2007.

[12] ISO 11783-2, "Tractors and machinery for agriculture and forestry - Serial control and communications data network," Part 2: Physical layer, International Organization for Standardization, 2002.

[13] ISO 11783-3, "Tractors and machinery for agriculture and forestry - Serial control and communications data network," Part 3: Data link layer, International Organization for Standardization, 2007.

[14] ISO 11783-4, "Tractors and machinery for agriculture and forestry - Serial control and communications data network," Part 4: Network layer, International Organization for Standardization, 2001.

[15] ISO 11783-5, "Tractors and machinery for agriculture and forestry - Serial control and communications data network," Part 5: Network management, International Organization for Standardization, 2007.

[16] ISO 11783-6, "Tractors and machinery for agriculture and forestry - Serial control and communications data network," Part 6: Virtual terminal, International Organization for Standardization, 2004.

[17] P. Fellmeth, "CAN-based tractor-agricultural implement communication ISO 11783," CAN Newsletter, vol. 9, 2003.

[18] AGCO Corporation. FieldStar, the Science of Agriculture, Virtual Terminal User's Guide. Publication No. 79015206 (English), February 2002, Duluth, GA.

[19] AGRCOM Gmbh and Agrarsystrem KG. CEBIS MOBILE VA User Guide. Manual (English). 2009, Bielefeld, Germany.

[20] DICKEY-John Corporation. Auto Section Control System, Operator's manual. Publication No. 11001-1561B-201207 (English). 2012, Auburn, IL, USA.

[21] Deere and Company. GreenStar 3 Display 2630 operator's manual. Publication No. OMPFP12408 (English). 2012, California, USA.

[22] Müller-Elektronik GmbH. ISOBUS-Terminals flexible and future-proof through APP & GO. 10/11. 2012, Salzkotten, Germany

[23] Yakin Liu, Xiaodong Cheng "Design and Implementation of Embedded Web Server Based on ARM and Linux" 2nd international Conference on Industrial Mechatnonics and Automation, 2010.

[24] Douglas, "Engineering Web Technologies for Embedded Applications," IEEE Internet Computing, May/June 1998.

[25] J. Dwight, M. Erwin, R. Niles, CGI Development Handbook. Machinery Industry Press.

[26] Freescale Semiconductor "User interface design using CGI programming and Boa web server on M5249C3 board", application note, 2006

[27] Jianmin Wang, Haibo Wei, "The transplantation of Boa Based on Linux3.0.1 and S3C6410", Telkomnika, Vol 11, 6, pp 3259-3264.

International Accreditation on Bachelor's and Master's Degree programmes

Sergelen Byambaa
Power Engineering School
Mongolian University of Science and
Technology
Ulaanbaatar, Mongolia
bsergelen@must.edu.mn

Batchimeg Tserenchoijil
Power Engineering School
Mongolian University of Science and
Technology
Ulaanbaatar, Mongolia
bch_509110@yahoo.com

Angar Sharkhuu
Power Engineering School
Mongolian University of Science and
Technology
Ulaanbaatar, Mongolia
angarsh@yahoo.com

Abstract – This paper describes short report of case in international accreditation system in Mongolia. The Power Engineering School (PES) of Mongolian University of Science and Technology (MUST) passed international accreditation by ASIIN, first time in our university. The quality of education system became more and more important not only in locally it is ghlighting in international level, too. To ensure quality of the programs by international high level accreditation is the one main measure of the evaluation of higher education. The "Electrical power supply" Bachelor's and Master's Degree programmes of PES successful evaluated by ASIIN, German accreditation center. Our further challenge is to proof one year accreditation further five years validity.

Keywords—ASIIN, EUR-ACE ,MUST, DEGREE accreditation, electrical Power Supply, programme, students

I. INTRODUCTION

In order to prepare Engineering and technology specialists Mongolia, Mongolian National University has started fering Industrial economics, construction engineering study programmes since 1959 and Geology and Power engineering study programmes since 1960. MUST has grown into a recognized higher education institution with 13 schools, e-hool, 2 polytechnic colleges, 1 TVET, 3 institutes, 51 enters, 1330 lecturers, 1019 employers and 3 high schools, ore than 30 000 students and became one of the leading omplex organization in the fields of science and technology.

MUST is the biggest University of Mongolia, providing quality education and research activities in the fields of echnique and technology of Mongolia, we thrive to prepare killed professionals, researchers, improve the operational quality and reputation, provide real opportunities, benefit from e positive outcomes and effectively use.

he MUST and the international higher education accreditation agency ASIIN e.V, European accreditation agency EUR-ACE have a good cooperation. Their experience, recommendations and providing their valuable advice help rengthen our higher education institutions in their quest to eet international standards.

I. ACTIVITIES

MUST mission: To prepare skilled professionals, researchers who are able compete internationally and domestically by understanding the market demand and provide consistent, quality, effective service that plays important role in economical development of the country by providing students with an opportunity to develop intellectual capital based on knowledge and innovation.

The aim of Bachelor degree program on Electrical power supply is to prepare the electrical engineering specialist in internationally recognized level, who had gained the theoretical and practical knowledge of installation and optimal operation of electrical and energy facilities and equipment which are necessary for supplying the energy consumers with reliable and high quality electrical energy. Graduated students of Electrical Supply programme are: to

have certain knowledge on the computer applications, automation of technology and business administration, able to continue next step of higher education – master

degree study in foreign language, to have a passion for self-advancement, and to have the academic and technical higher education level of which general qualification profiles laid down at national and international level, meeting the European higher education requirements (EUR-ACE label-3).

From the academic year 2012-2013 we have enroll students for 2+2 dual program as MOA between Electrical Supply program prepared by Electrical supply and High Voltage engineering professor's team and North China Electric Power University.

Also from the this academic year was implementing the Project of teaching (in English) the subjects bachelors and masters degree studying by lectures of Czech Technical University in Prague at the professors team of Electrical Supply and High Voltage Engineering, School of Power Engineering of Mongolian Technical University in Ulaanbaatar.

In the year 2013, ASIIN e.V. and EUR-ACE approved the accreditation of the Electric Power Supply Engineering program of the Power Engineering School of MUST. This accreditation was not only the first step toward our long-term goal of becoming an internationally recognized, research based open-university, but it has also formed the basis for our institution's future success, development and progress.

The international higher education accreditation agency ASIIN e.V. and European higher education agency EUR-ACE has accredited more than 2,000 institutions not only in Europe but also in the Americas, Africa and Asia. This track record clearly demonstrates their reputation and credibility.

Many thousands of students, beginning from our forefathers up to the present day have studied in educational institutions in Europe; a cradle of brilliant scientific discoveries and achievements. These Mongolian students have returned to contribute to the development, progress and welfare of their motherland. The pathways connecting Europe with Mongolian education will be paved and widened in future.

The accreditation by ASIIN e.V. will serve as a powerful engine of change for the on-going development of MUST and Mongolia's magnificence as a nation.

ASIIN e. V. is a registered association in accordance with the law of the Federal Republic of Germany.

The association is supported by many organisations, which view the quality of university education as a central concern. They are associations of universities and universities of applied sciences, expert societies, profession-related organisations, industrial and business associations and unions. This alliance was first founded in 1999 as the non-profit association ASIIN for the accreditation of degree programmes in engineering an informatics, which rapidly expanded to ASIIN in 2002 by including the fields of natural sciences and mathematics.

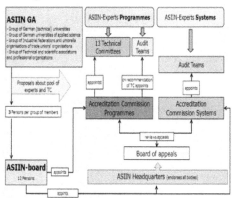

Fig. 1. The structure of ASIIN e. V.

The ASIIN General Criteria describe
- The principles according to which the accreditation procedures are designed
- The requirements for the accreditation of degree programmes.

The ASIIN General Criteria is subject to critical review or regular basis and adapted to current developments and resu from accreditation practice.

Within the programme accreditation, ASIIN e. V. speciali in revising and certifying Bachelor's and Master's deg programmes:
- In engineering
- In computer science
- In the natural sciences
- In mathematics
- In all interdisciplinary areas which include one the aforementioned subject areas
- In international and European cooperation, e "double degree" or "joint degree", which inclu one of the aforementioned subject areas
- In teacher training programmes

Currently, the Netherlands, Switzerland, China and the A countries, such as Kazakhstan, included in the accreditati programme.

The 'Electrical Supply and High Volta Engineering" professor's team of MUST has included additional self –assessment report, Module handbook a Matrixes which can demonstrate our last 2 years academ training process on Bachelor's and Master's Degree for profession of "Electrical Power Supply" according to ASI e.V. accreditation 7 requirements and recommendations the different seals.

In the year 2013, ASIIN / EUR-ACE approved accreditation of the "Electric Power Supply" Engineeri programme of the Power Engineering School of Mongol University of Science and Technology.

MUST and ASIIN organized "Internatio Accreditation & Quality Assurance "Joint-Seminar" in the 29 of January, 2015, in Ulaanbaatar, Mongolia.

The international higher education accreditati agency ASIIN and EUR-ACE as well as officials a internationally recognized experts for visiting and shari their experience and providing their valuable advice to MUS Their recommendations were strengthen our higher educati institutions in their quest to meet international standards.

It will be successful way in the future, as we have started fro the beginning in order to evaluate our the results of our ha work to fulfill the academic training needs on pov engineering, especially on electrical engineering for varic sectors of infrastructure and community of Mongolia basi on our existing experience and real results. We have tried write the additional self- assessment report, which was accordance to the ASIIN rule and recommendations. In t report, we include the additional self –assessment repc Module handbook and Matrixes which can demonstrate c last 2 years educational (or academic) training process Bachelor's and Master's Degree for the profession "Electrical Power Supply" according to ASIIN accreditatio requirements and recommendations for the different seals.

Many thousands of students, beginning from our forefath up to the present day have studied in educational institutic in Europe; a cradle of brilliant scientific discoveries a achievements. These Mongolian students have returned to contribute to the development, progress and welfare of their motherland. The pathways connecting Europe with Mongolian education will be paved and widened from the contributions garnered from this accreditation.

Therefore, we have been facing the confidence for being accredited our Bachelor's and Master's Degree Programmes for 5 years by ASIIN – one of world known organization on Technical Higher Education Accreditation.

We really appreciate their noble deed for checking our additional self-assessment report of the Bachelor's and Master's Degree Programmes in "Electrical power supply" conducted at Mongolian University of Science and Technology.

Table I. Teacher's and Institutional training activity of Electrical Engineering Department of PES, MUST

№	Teacher's & Institutional training activity	2012-2013year 189 students	2013-2014year 189 students
1	Training load is adequate to understand the curriculum	3.44	3.7
2	Teacher's teaching skill is adequate	4.01	4.2
3	Teacher's consult with students in extracurricular time	3.44	3.7
4	Teacher's give adequate time for students individual work	3.52	3.9
5	Teacher's use adequate textbook & teaching aids for use in lessons	3.48	3.7
6	Institution provides student services in a timely fashion (performance report, tuition fees, etc.)	3.48	3.6
7	Institution supplies appropriate training equipment	3.93	4
8	Due to International Accreditation in the field of Electrical power Supply did training qualities improve?		3.9
9	Average score of evaluation	3.61	3.8

Table II. Training and learning environment of Electrical Engineering Department of PES, MUST

№	Training and learning environment	2012-2013 year 189 students	2013-2014 year 185 students
1	The convenience & condition of the training area (auditorium & office)	3.45	3.7
2	Use of equipment & laboratory conditions	4.05	4.2
3	Library service at MUST	3.77	4.1
4	Do the Student Council's activities support students?	2.81	3.1
5	What's your idea about the school cafeteria?	2.77	3.1
6	Cloakroom service?	2.59	3.1
7	Institution supplies appropriate training equipment	3.93	4
8	Due to the International Accreditation in the field of Electric Power Supply, did the school facilities improve?		3.7
9	Average score of evaluation	3.24	3.6

Graduated students GPA of Electrical power supply study programme of PES, MUST

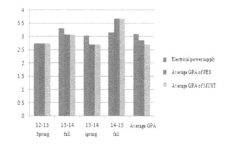

Fig. 2. Graduate students' GPA of "Electrical power supply" study programme

Fig. 1. Graduate students' GPA of "Electrical power supply" study programme in the Electrical Engineering department compared with the graduate students' GPA at PES.

As a direct consequence of accreditation, the academic programmes in Electrical power supply have garnered an increased level of recognition both in Mongolia and abroad. The number domestic and international applicants for bachelor and master degree programmes are increasing.

Graduates from other Mongolian universities are increasingly interested in applying for PES precisely thanks to its reputation gained from the accreditation.

Specific results from the internationally accredited electrical power supply programmes can be summarized as follows:

1. A joint course will be organized with the Czech Technical University in "electrical engineering".

2. The school is improving its syllabus / curriculum by drawing upon the content of Austrian international training modules.

3. A joint programme with a Korean University is under development. This includes a Bachelor's degree 2+2 programme and a 1+1 Master's degree programme.

4. A joint programme with a Japanese university is being developed for a 2+2 Bachelor's degree programme.

5. A joint programme with a Chinese university for the delivery of a 2+2 Bachelor's degree programme is also under development.

6. The Novosibirsk Technical University is working with MUST for the delivery of a 1+1 joint Bachelor's degree programme.

II. CONCLUSION

- The "Electrical Power Supply" Engineering programme of the Power Engineering School of Mongolian University of Science and Technology has a good result of the requirements below the ASIIN –(Accreditation

Agency for Degree Programmes in Engineering, Informatics, the Natural Sciences and Mathematics):

- Many thousands of students, beginning from our forefathers up to the present day have studied in educational institutions in Europe; a cradle of brilliant scientific discoveries and achievements.
- These Mongolian students have returned to contribute to the development, progress and welfare of their motherland.
- Therefore, we have been facing the confidence for being accredited Electrical power supply Bachelor's and Master's Degree Programmes for 5 years by ASIIN e.V. -one of world known organization on Technical Higher Education Accreditation.

- This accreditation was not only the first step toward our long-term goal of becoming an internationally recognized, research based open-university, but it has also formed the basis for our institution's future success, development and progress.
- The findings indicate that the students' entire questionnaire answers in 2013-2014 shown positive than academic year 2012-2013. This result relates to institutional work and activities for International Accreditation of Electrical Power Supply in last two years. Based on the questionnaire comments, we planned some activities in the academic year 2012-2013.

- As far as students' feedback, 12% considered that it is necessary to have accreditation for Electrical Power Supply and Electric System majors. According to the survey, it was very significant for the school to solve the problems related to the number of seats in the library, availability of textbooks and on the job training practical activities and duration, because these were mentioned again in both questionnaires in academic years 2012-2013 and 2013-2014.

REFERENCES

[1] www.asiin.de
[2] ECTS Users Guide 2009
[3] http://must.edu.mn
[4] Workshop material on "International Accreditation and Quality Assurance" in MUST, 2015
[5] www.**asiin**-ev.de/pages/en.php
[6] www.akkreditierungsrat.de/index.
[7] https://www.fer.unizg.hr/en/about/**asiin**
[8] www.**asiin**-consult.de/
[9] www.res.edu.mn

The E-Learning and Virtual Laboratory in Engineering Education on The Example of MUST

Uranchimeg Tudevdagva

Power Engineering School, Mongolian University of Science and Technology
Ulaanbaatar, Mongolia

Abstract – **This paper deals about e-learning and virtual laboratory development in engineering education system. The example of the facts based on the Mongolian University of Science and Technology (MUST). The one of the biggest university MUST giving high attention to quality of the teaching. To support professors and lecturers by teaching environment the MUST started to deal with e-courses and virtual laboratories. E-courses and virtual laboratories are good tools for teaching and the MUST supports this type of tools in teaching.**

From this paper you can read actual statistical facts about MUST and e-learning in MUST. Further planning and development of elearning and virtual laboratories in MUST.

Keywords—e-learning; virtual laboratory; engineering education, MUST, e-tools.

I. INTRODUCTION

In an era of new technological developments, e-learning has become a central issue in future developments of education systems. E-learning is widely being used in conventional, continuing, adult education and corporate training because of its exibility, richness, resource-sharing, and cost-effectiveness [1]. United Nations Educational, Scientific and Cultural Organization (UNESCO) statistics show that over 455 million people around the world had received education and training through the Internet in 2008. Over 70% of universities in USA were providing e-learning courses, and more than 6.1 million university students were taking at least one e-learning course during the fall 2010 term, which accounted for over 31% of the total number of university students in USA [2].

The Mongolian University of Science and Technology (MUST) is center for Mongolian engineering education. It is a multidisciplinary and multi level university for education, training and scientific research. The MUST is also one of the largest centers for scientific and cultural exchanges in Mongolia. MUST is one of the first universities in Mongolia which included e-learning methods into higher education [1].

E-learning by own characteristics and opportunity opens many new views and tools in teaching for faculty. Different type of the e-learning help professors and lecturers to teach difficult engineering theories and topics with new manner and with new methods. One of the main type of the e-tools is virtual laboratory. Virtual laboratories play major roles in engineering education.

The MUST is the one of the first university where faculty trying to create virtual laboratories and use them for teaching and learning in engineering education.

In 2010, the Information Technology Centre and ICT Teaching Methodological Centre were joined on the basis of Order No. 183 of Minister of Education, Culture and Science and according to Order No. 28 of the Rector, E-Open School was founded to administrate distance-learning activities of the University and it has been working with below structure since January, 2010 [3]:

- Training & Teaching Methodological Team
- Information Technology & Software Team
- Internet & Hardware Team
- Online Testing room
- U-CLASS distanced-learning room
- Online & Video Conference hall
- Multimedia Studio with full equipment

This school today offering many e-courses and advanced training courses. For example [3]:

Main courses

- E-Courses for Bachelor Degree
- E-Courses for Master Degree
- E-Courses for Doctor Degree

Advanced Training

- E-Courses for Bachelor Degree
- E-Courses for Master Degree
- E-Courses for Doctor Degree
- Programming technology training
- Database training
- Network technology training
- Computer graphics training
- Special advanced training
- Training to improve information technology skills of the lecturers and student of the Mongolian University of Science and Technology
- Curriculum training for lecturers

- To improve information technology skills
- To prepare E-Courses
- Curriculum training for students
- To improve information technology skills
- Qualification

II. THE MUST FACTS

In current days in MUST studying, 16486 undergraduate, 1892 graduated and 444 doctor students.

In 2007 the university started to offer web based distance learning courses for master students (see Table 1). Figure 1 shows that the interest in e-learning courses at MUST has increased very substantially since 2007 [1].

TABLE I. E-learning in MUST

Academic year	Term	E-Students	E-Courses
2007/2008	Spring	62	19
2008/2009	Autumn	81	8
2008/2009	Spring	59	13
2009/2010	Autumn	116	20
2009/2010	Spring	113	20
2010/2011	Autumn	251	23
2010/2011	Spring	447	43
2011/2012	Autumn	532	71
2011/2012	Spring	976	124
2012/2013	Autumn	1205	150
2012/2013	Spring	904	161
2013/2014	Autumn	1181	211

For the first time this e-learning opportunity of studying while working. The MUST uses its own learning management system (LMS) Unimis, which manage all its online courses. supports e-learning by an own learning management system, the Unimis system.

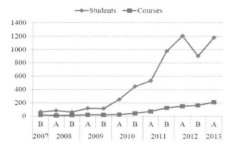

Fig. 1. E-learning in MUST

All online courses are managed by this LMS. Students which want to attend an e-learning course have to enroll via Unimis system. The Unimis system is an e-learning framework which supports students and tutors at administration processes. The LMS has data bases for e-contents, students and tutors.

Today in data base of the e-courses we have 149 bachelor 229 master, totally 378 topics. Since 2013 number of e-course increased by 167. Obce more confirmation about e-learning development in MUST is by last two years we received 16 new topics in e-version.

III. VIRTUAL LABORATORY AND ITS EVALUATION

The Virtual laboratory started to take attention very early i education system. In early virtual laboratories used as usual i chemical and physical topics in secondary schools. Later i became very famous in higher education system, too.

A request to create and update different laboratories i MUST is increasing from year to year relating to technologica and technical development of fields. To build new laboratorie for teaching and research is always has financial problems i developing countries. To fit requirement of the students and jo givers we have to solve this laboratory need problem.

One of the main solution for this is to create and use virtua laboratories in teaching. Since 2010 Power Engineering Schoo of MUST started testing project to create virtual laboratory [4] First version of the virtual laboratory was developed fo computer science in Power engineering school (PES). Use this virtual laboratory for traditional teaching like e-tool fo teaching from 2010 to 2014. After usage of virtual laboratorie we did evaluation by structure oriented evaluation model [1].

Fig. 2. Logical structure of evaluation for virtual laboratory

Figure 2 shows key logical structure of evaluation mode for first virtual laboratory in PES. After definition of key goal defined sub goals and created checklist (Fig.3).

Key	Sub	Questions	disagree 0	1	2	3	agree 4	5
		Content quality						
B1	A11	Content objectives was clearly defined						
	A12	Content level met my expectation						
	A13	Content was designed well						
		Design quality						
B2	A21	Design of usability was well						
	A22	Virtual laboratory general design was good						
		Tutor skill						
B3	A31	Tutors was supportive in virtual learning environment						
	A32	Tutors feedback during study was helpful						
		User communication interface						
B4		User communication interface was designed easy to use						
	A41	and understand						
		Self assessment quality						
B5		Self assessment was good organized and well related to						
	A51	content						
		Virtual study environment						
B6	A61	Collaborative learning environment was useful to study						
	A62	Virtual room for learners was helpful during study						
		Learning support environment						
B7	A71	Introduction had well organized full information						
	A72	Practical part of virtual laboratory was supportive for study						
		Learning support environment had well organized tools						
	A73	between tutor and learner						
		Practical reality						
B8		Practical reality was developed well nearly to real						
	A81	environment						

Fig. 3. The checklist of evaluation for virtual laboratory

By this checklist collected data from students who us virtual laboratories in learning.

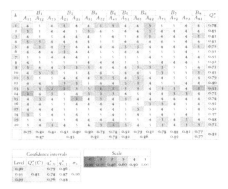

Fig. 4. Collected and processed data of evaluation

Maximum value of the evaluation was 1,00. By evaluation data we can see that virtual laboratory quality was measured like 0.82. The confidence interval for this value is 0.10. From this evaluation we can summarize the usage of the virtual laboratory is very important in higher education and students are welcoming this type of teaching.

Today we have 14 virtual laboratories in different schools of MUST. The need of the virtual laboratory is increasing from year to year. In 2011 started small project in PES of MUST for virtual laboratory. By first part of this project created 8 modules of virtual laboratories for 8 different topics and one all virtual laboratory. Now we are looking to fund to continue this project.

CONCLUSION

The e-learning and virtual laboratory are one of the main direction of modern education system. We have to fit expectation of the students in technological era. To support development and usage of e-learning have to be highlighted policy of each higher education organization.

To create and update virtual laboratory we need to have permanent team with professional persons. For this MUST have to include in the global plan of MUST special policy and issue which focused to development of e-learning and virtual laboratories. We have support this type of activity to fit expectation of the students and to support professors and lecturers. By evaluation of students and by discussion of professors we can conclude that e-learning and virtual laboratory is the leading tools and direction in modern education systems.

REFERENCES

[1] Uranchimeg Tudevdagva, "Structure oriented evaluation model for e-learning", Wissenschaftliche Schriftenreihe, Eingebettete, Selbstorganisierende Systeme, Vol. 14, Chemnitz, Germany, 2014, pp.4.

[2] Weiss, C., H. "The Interface Between Evaluation and Public Policy, in Evaluation: The International Journal of Theory, Research, and Practice", Vol.5 N.4, 1999. pp.468-486. (http://evi.sagepub.com/content/5/4/468.full.pdf+html)

[3] E-open school of MUST, Information web site, Online avalaible: http://www.must.edu.mn/must_en/modules.php?R_Id=28

[4] Uranchimeg Tudevdagva, Ayush Yumchmaa, Baatar Batshagai, "The virtual laboratories case study in traditional teaching and e-learning for engineering sceinces", In proceedings of Ubi-Media Computing and Workshops (UMEDIA), 2014 7th International Conference, 2014, pp.281-285.

MOOC from The View of Students

Oyudari Lkha-Ochir
National University of Mongolia
Ulaanbaatar, Mongolia
Oyuk_lkh@yahoo.com

Nomindari Lkha-Ochir
Institute of Finance and Economics
Ulaanbaatar, Mongolia
Nomiko_nd@yahoo.com

Abstract – The confluence of technology and education is undoubtedly significant. As we navigate through intense change in education delivery and access, the road ahead can seem uncertain. This paper describes the some desireable purpose about mooc then ferocious things by massive open online course. A MOOC is an online course with the option of free and open registration, a publicly-shared curriculum, and open-ended outcomes. MOOCs integrate social networking, accessible online resources, and are facilitated by leading practitioners in the field of study. And I think that it is useful for students for practice.

Keywords:MOOC, student view, online learning, masiive learning.

I. Inroduction

What is the MOOC? A massive open online course (MOOC) is an online course aimed at unlimited participation and open access via the web. In addition to traditional course materials such as filmed lectures, readings, and problem sets, many MOOCs provide interactive user forums to support community interactions between students, professors, and teaching assistants. MOOCs are a recent and widely researched development in distance education[1] which was first introduced in 2008 and emerged as a popular mode of learning in 2012[2][3].

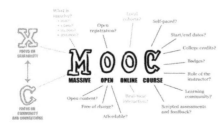

II. Online learning at school helps prepare teens for university

Online learning has been around for more than 30 years, but recent excitement around Massive Open Online Courses (MOOCs) has brought it fully into the public eye. In schools, online learning used to be a remedial alternative to classroom teaching, particularly where learners were geographically dispersed. But there is a growing belief that it might offer all students some distinct experiences that can prepare them for higher education.

There is a growing interest in the possibilities that different forms of virtual schooling can offer. This isn't about whether online learning is better or worse than conventional teaching. As a 2009 US Department for Education report demonstrated, decades of research on "media effects" still shows no conclusive evidence that either approach leads to improved learning outcomes.

There is evidence that learners who study both online and in schools benefit because they spend additional time learning and are given tasks and materials not received by pupils studying face-to-face. It is not simply because of the medium of study.

So what are the benefits? A study by the Institute of Education explored the experiences of current university students who had completed the International Baccalaureate Diploma Programme (IBDP). The IBDP includes online courses designed and delivered by Pamoja Education[4]. There were 108 usable responses from students aged between 17 and 23, three-quarters of them women.

Students who had completed the online courses identified several benefits. Confidence with technology was one obvious advantage. Students who had studied online were familiar with technologies that formed an essential part of university life, such as virtual learning environments, discussion forums, Google tools, and audio-visual learning resources such as YouTube.

Of the students interviewed, 94% said finding academic resources on the internet was important to their success and 78% said being able to plan group tasks using online calendars, scheduling tools and discussion applications mattered. Another 71% found social networks useful for building relationships with other learners[5].

There were also cultural benefits. Online classes brought learners from other countries together: 36 countries were represented in the survey[6]. Learners valued exposure to different perspectives on issues. One student described how this experience online had helped them develop valuable skills and approaches: "I often use Google Docs and other Google tools to collaborate on group projects, including working with teams that are in different locations and time zones."

Perhaps most importantly, students who had studied online described how important it was that they could learn independently. They were less likely than their peers to rely on tutors for help and more likely to set goals based on their own performance rather other students'. They had also developed better strategies for managing and pacing their studies. One 21-year old student said:
Studying online is different from attending regular classes. You have to be self-motivated to study on your own and set your own deadlines. Personally, I learned a lot from taking an online course because it helped me prepare myself in terms of scheduling and allocating time to finish each of the subjects that I am currently taking.

III. Have MOOCs Helped or Hurt?

As the hype around MOOCs has subsided, a frequently asked question in university circles today is: Who have massive open online courses helped or hurt?

Providing free and open access to content from revered institutions is laudable. But enrollments at elite colleges' MOOCs do not translate into revenue at the vast majority of colleges and universities, many of them already cash-strapped. And learning that fails to deliver credit that leads to a credential may not yield much for students, even if they enjoy the courses. MOOCs may have been more faddish than altruistic.

PROS	CONS
SHOWS HAVE AN EXISTING, LOYAL FANBASE	NEGOTIATING WITH NETWORKS & STUDIOS MAY BE DIFFICULT
GAIN RIGHTS TO PREVIOUS SEASONS; POTENTIAL FOR SYNDICATION DEALS	SMALLER BUDGET COULD LEAD TO RESGINATIONS OR LAYOFFS OF CREW AND/OR CAST
NO NEED TO PRODUCE ENTIRE SERIES' FROM SCRATCH	AUDIENCE SIZE MAY BE TOO SMALL OR NICHE TO JUSTIFY INVESTMENT
USE SOCIAL MEDIA AND OTHER WEB TOOLS TO CREATE MORE ENGAGED AUDIENCES	

For MOOCs to be important long term, they must be more than a curiosity. A 2014 study from the University of Pennsylvania's Graduate School of Education found that only 4 percent of those who had registered for a MOOC actually completed it. The curious are obviously much less likely to see a course through to completion than are serious students seeking a credential to help them advance in their lives.

Studies like the one out of Penn suggest that MOOCs may have little long-term utility for students. And for institutions, the risks of issuing credit for MOOCs could have a serious impact on their operating income. Most of those who have created MOOCs have invested a lot of sweat equity in return for relatively little, and no meaningful income for provider universities that contributed their brand and reputation to support the concept.

At a time when many colleges and universities are struggling to justify their value proposition and find financial sustainability, marking their core product to zero seems to be misguided, an observation that is gaining currency among higher educators worldwide. This practice also raises a question whether free implies little value.

Giving away education can make sense in some cases. For instance, the country of Colombia, which has offered MOOC-like courses through SENA, its agency focused on providing practical and technical educational courses to increase employment, and India, which is considering putting high-demand courses online for workforce training may prove that free and open courses online can be effective in up-skilling societies.[7] It is important to keep in mind, however, that these initiatives are seen as a public good and, as such, are fully funded by the government and not by institutions that need to find their way to self-sufficiency.

Using technology to deliver relevant, affordable, and credential-bearing education from top universities to help more citizens progress in their lives is within the incredible potential of the Internet and can be done inexpensively and at scale, as MOOCs have demonstrated.

While the participation of top universities in the delivery of MOOCs has helped further legitimize online learning and infuse higher education with much needed innovation, it has not proven to be the anticipated game changer for either students or universities. History has shown us that giveaways are a gambler's game and not a strategy for a sustainable future.

IV.   My Problem With MOOCs

Giving college credit for a massive open online course will devalue degrees, but the moment I write that, a voice in my mind asks, "Why do you believe that?"

Although I don't think colleges and universities should equate MOOCs with other courses, I'm no Luddite. I'm happy to see digital humanities breathe life into literary studies, and at one point I took an online class to prepare to teach in that format. Since then I've taught several courses entirely online, but the results discouraged me: Committed students did well, but the rest did poorly or vanished.

Although some students have problems in my face-to-face classes, I'm able to intervene and provide help earlier in that format, so far fewer disappear. Currently I use digital resources to enhance the classes I teach, but I have no desire to run a course entirely online again. Therefore I assume that instructors who favor MOOCs have taught online classes with quality equal to or better than their face-to-face classes.

I associate the voice in my head so closely with the flesh-and-blood individual that I cannot imagine a MOOC having a similar lifelong effect, but I give the MOOCs a pass on this one because they haven't been around long enough for anyone to determine their long-term influence.

MOOCs are becoming acceptable in higher education because people richer and more powerful than I am declare them to be good. I still expect

MOOCs to devalue the worth of degrees, I have a better understanding of why I believe what I do.

And I understood many things from this video by GeorgeSiemens.
https://www.youtube.com/watch?v=-a2cEzsMEMY

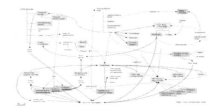

A network diagram showing the distributive nature of Stephen Downes' and George Siemens' CCK08 course, one of the first MOOCs and the course that inspired the term MOOC to become adopted.[7]

V.   Conclusion

However, open licensing and open source is not the be-all and end-all. As previously discussed, all of these aspects of "open" tie into the aspect of being "open involvement". Byopening their doors to more user participation and involvement at every level of their MOOC projects, providers will greatly benefit for the reasons mentioned above and help further the goals of open education. Through our evaluation of the top six MOOC providers on the basis of four aspects of openness: enrollment, licensing, platform, and involvement, we wereintroduced to the values a culture of openness can bring. By establishing such a culture and being pragmatically open, MOOC enterprises have nothing to lose and everything to gain. In their current shape and form, massive online classes have issues that prevent them from really makinga dent in the predominant education paradigm. Truly disrupting the status quo requires them tonot just transfer current models online, but transform them. The MOOCs hype bubble will burst unless they become more than just open in enrollment. They need to live up totheir moniker and become massive and truly open online courses.

References

[1] International Review of Research in Open and Distributed Learning, 16(1),330-363. https://www.academia.edu/11056576/Trends_in_Distance_Education_Research_A_Content_Analysis_of_Journals_2009-2013

[2] Pappano, Laura. "The Year of the MOOC". The New York Times. Retrieved 18 April 2014.

[3] Lewin, Tamar. "Universities Abroad Join Partnerships on the Web". *New York Times*. Retrieved 6 March 2013.

[4] "A brief guide to understanding MOOCs". *The Internet Journal of Medical Education*

[5] "What You Need to Know About MOOCs". Chronicle of Higher Education. Retrieved 14 March 2013

[6] "Open Education for a global economy".

[7] Downes, Stephen (2008). "CCK08 - The Distributed Course". The MOOC Guide. Retrieved 11 September 2013.